Next time you want to learn about something, try googling your nearest bookshop.

Waterstones

GRANTA

12 Addison Avenue, London W11 4QR | email editorial@granta.com
To subscribe go to www.granta.com, or call 845-267-3031 (toll-free 866-438-6150)
in the United States, 020 8955 7011 in the United Kingdom

ISSUE 126: WINTER 2014

PUBLISHER AND ACTING EDITOR	Sigrid Rausing
MANAGING EDITOR	Yuka Igarashi
ONLINE EDITOR	Rachael Allen
ASSISTANT DESIGNER	Daniela Silva
PUBLICITY	Aidan O'Neill
MARKETING AND SUBSCRIPTIONS	David Robinson
EDITORIAL ASSISTANTS	Louise Scothern, Francisco Vilhena
TO ADVERTISE CONTACT	Kate Rochester, katerochester@granta.com
FINANCE	Morgan Graver
SALES	Iain Chapple, Katie Hayward
IT MANAGER	Mark Williams
PRODUCTION ASSOCIATE	Sarah Wasley
PROOFS	David Atkinson, Francine Brody, Katherine Fry, Vimbai Shire
CONTRIBUTING EDITORS	Daniel Alarcón, Mohsin Hamid, Isabel Hilton, Blake Morrison, John Ryle, Edmund White

CONTENTS

CHRIS ADRIAN · AYANA MATHIS · JACKSON TAYLOR · DANYEL SMITH · JUSTIN TORRES · TAYLOR PLIMPTON

THE WRITER'S FOUNDRY MFA

to be, not to seem.

St. Joseph's College
NEW YORK

www.sjcny.edu/mfa

THE INDIAN UPRISING

Ann Beattie

'There's no copyright on titles,' he said. 'It wouldn't be a good idea, probably, to call something "Death of a Salesman", but you could do it.'

'I wanted to see the play, but it was sold out. Tickets were going for $1,500 at the end of the run. I did get to New York and go to the Met, though, and paid my two dollars to get in.'

'Two dollars is nicer than one dollar,' he said.

'Ah! So you do care what people think!'

'Don't talk like you're using exclamation points,' he said. 'It doesn't suit people who are intelligent. You've been fighting your intelligence for a long time, but exclaiming is the coward's way of undercutting yourself.'

'Cynicism's better?'

'I wonder why I've created so many adversaries,' he said, then did a good Randy Travis imitation. 'I got friends in . . . high places . . .'

'Maker's Mark interests you more than anyone, every time. We used to come see you and we have a burning desire to talk to you, to pick your brain, find out what to read, make you smile, but by the end of every evening, it's clear who's your best friend.'

'But pity me: I have to pay for that best friend. We don't have an unlimited calling plan.'

'How can you still have so much ego involved that you hate it that my father's company pays for my cellphone and doesn't – what? Send someone to come rake your leaves for free?'

'The super does that. He doesn't have a rake, though. He refuses to think the maple's gotten as big as it has. Every year, he's out there with the broom and one black garbage bag.'

'Made for a good poem,' I said.

'Thank you,' he said seriously. 'I was wondering if you'd seen it.'

'We all subscribe to everything. Unless we're as broke as I'd be without my daddy, as you so often point out.'

'If the maple starts to go, the super will be thrilled, and as a good citizen, I promise to chop and burn the wood in the WBF, not let it be made into paper. Paper is so sad. Every sheet, a thin little tombstone.'

'How's Rudolph?'

'Rudolph is energetic again, since the vet's found a substitute for the pills that made him sleep all the time. I envied him, but that's what the old envy: sleep.'

'Is this the point where I try to convince you seventy isn't old?'

'I've got a better idea. I'm about to turn seventy-one, so why don't you get Daddy to fly you here and we can celebrate my birthday at the same restaurant where Egil Fray shot the bottle of tequila, then offered the bartender a slice of lime as it poured down from the top shelf like a waterfall. Egil was funny.'

Egil, back in college, had been the star student of our class: articulate; irreverent; devoted to books; interested in alcohol, bicycling, Italian cooking, UFOs and Apple stock. He'd been diagnosed bipolar after he dove off the Delaware Memorial Bridge and broke every rib, his nose and one wrist, and said he was sorry he'd had the idea. That was years ago, when he'd had insurance, when he was still married to Brenda, when everybody thought he was the brightest boy, including his doctors. He'd gotten good with a slingshot – none of that macho shooting the apple off the wife's head – but he'd caused a significant amount of damage, even when taking good aim. He was finishing medical school now.

I said, 'I wonder if that's a sincere wish.'

'It would be great,' he said, and for a second I believed him, until he filled in the details: 'You'd be in your hotel room on your cellphone, and I'd be here with my man Rudy, talking to you from the Princess phone.'

He really did have a Princess phone, and he was no more wrong about that than Egil had been about Apple. Repairmen had offered him serious money for the pale blue phone. His ex-wife (Carrie, his third, the only one I'd known) had asked for it officially, in court papers – along with half his frequent-flyer miles, from the days when he devotedly visited his mother in her Colorado nursing home.

'You know, it would be good to see you,' I said. 'I can afford a ticket. What about next Monday? What are you doing then?'

'Getting ready for Halloween. Looking in every drawer for my rubber fangs.'

'Can't help you there, but I could bring my Groucho glasses and moustache.'

'I'll take you to the finest new restaurant,' he said. 'My favourite item on the menu is "Pro and Pros". It's a glass of prosecco and some very delicious hard cheese wrapped in prosciutto. Alcoholics don't care about entrées.'

'Then we go dancing?' (We *had* gone dancing; we had, we had, we had. Everyone knew it, and every woman envied me.)

'I don't think so, unless you just wanted to dance around the floor with me held over your head, like Mel Fisher on the floor of the ocean with his buried treasure, or a goat you'd just killed.'

'You live in Philadelphia, not Greece.'

'There is no more Greece,' he said. 'They fucked themselves good.'

Pretty soon thereafter, he had a coughing fit and my boyfriend came into the kitchen with raised eyebrows meant to ask: Are you sleeping with me tonight? and we hung up.

I took the train. It wasn't difficult. I got a ride with a friend to some branch of Metro going into Washington and rode it to Union Station. Then I walked forever down the train track to a car someone finally let me on. I felt like an ant that had walked the length of a caterpillar's body and ended up at its anus. I sat across from a mother with a small son whose head she abused any time she got bored looking out the window: swatting it with plush toys; rearranging his curls; inspecting him for nits.

The North 34th Street station was familiar, though the photo booth was gone. We'd had our pictures taken there, a strip of them, and we'd fought over who got them, and then after I won, I lost them somehow. I went outside and splurged on a cab.

Since his divorce, Franklin had lived in a big stone building with a curving driveway. At first, as the cab approached, I thought there might be a hitching post, but it turned out to be a short man in a red vest with his hair slicked back. He took an older man's hand, and the two set off, waved forward by the cabbie.

This was great, I thought; I didn't have to worry about parking, I'd gotten money from a cash machine before the trip and wouldn't have to think about that until I ran short at the end of the month, and here I was, standing in front of the imposing building where my former teacher lived. Inside, I gave the woman behind the desk his name and mine. She had dark purple fingernails and wore many bracelets. 'Answer, hon, answer,' she breathed into her phone, flicking together a couple of nails. 'This is Savannah, sending you her "answer" jujus.'

Finally he did pick up, and she said my name, listened so long that I thought Franklin might be telling her a joke, then said, 'All right, hon,' hung up and gave me a Post-it note with 303 written on it that I hadn't asked for. I sent him Royal Riviera pears every Christmas, books from Amazon, Virginia peanuts, and hell, it wasn't the first time I'd visited, either. I knew his apartment number.

Though the hallway looked different. That was because (I was about to find out) someone very rich had been irritated at the width of the corridors and had wanted to get his antique car into his living room, so he'd paid to widen the hallway, which had created a god-awful amount of dust, noise and inconvenience.

It was funnier in Franklin's telling. We clinked shot glasses (mine brimming only with white wine), called each other Russian names and tossed down the liquor. If everything we said had been a poem, the index of first lines would have formed a pattern: 'Do you remember', 'Tell me if I remember wrong', 'There was that time', 'Wasn't it funny when'.

When I looked out the window, I saw that it had begun to snow. Rudolph had been the first to see it, or to sense it; he'd run to the window and put his paws on the ledge, tail aquiver.

'I hated it when I was a kid and this happened. My mother made me wear my winter jacket over my Halloween costume and that ruined everything. Who's going to know what gender anybody is supposed to be under their Barbour jacket, let alone their exact identity?'

'The receptionist,' he said, 'is a guy who became a woman. He had the surgery in Canada because it was a lot cheaper. He had saline bags put in for tits, but then he decided flat-chested women were sexy, so he had them taken out. I asked for one, to put in a jar, but no go: you'd have thought I was asking for a foetus.'

The bottle of bourbon was almost full. We might be sitting for a long time, I realized. I said, 'Let's go get something to eat before the snow piles up. How far would we have to go to get to that restaurant?'

'You're afraid if we stay here, I'll have more to drink and try to seduce you.'

'No I'm not,' I said indignantly.

'You're afraid I'll invite Savannah to come with us and give us all the gory details. Savannah is a former Navy SEAL.'

'If you like it when I speak in a monotone, don't tell me weird stuff.'

'Listen to her! When the only buttons I ever push are for the elevator. I don't live by metaphor, woman. Don't you read the critics?'

He kicked his shoes out from behind the footstool. Good – so he was game. His ankles didn't look great, but at least they were shoes I'd have to get on his feet, not cowboy boots, and they seemed to have sturdy treads. I knelt and picked up one foot, opened the Velcro fastener and used my palm as a shoehorn. His foot slid in easily. On the other foot, though, the arch, as well as the ankle, was swollen, but we decided it would work fine if the fastener was left open. It was a little problem to keep the Velcro from flipping over and fastening itself, but I folded the top strap and held it together with a big paper clip, and eventually we got going.

'An old man like me, and I've got no scarf, no hat, only gloves I bought from a street vendor, the same day I had a roasted chestnut and bought another one for a squirrel. I can tell you which one of us was happier.' He was holding the crook of my arm. 'Only you would take me out in the snow for a meal. Promise me one thing: you won't make me watch you make a snowball and throw it in a wintery way. You can make an anecdote of that request and use it later at my memorial service.'

He'd had a triple bypass two years before. He had diabetes. He'd told me on the phone that he might have to go on dialysis.

'Is this the part of the walk where you tell me how your relationship is with that fellow I don't consider my equal?'

'Did I bring him up?' I said.

'No, I did. So is he still not my equal?'

'I feel disloyal talking about him. He lost his job. He hasn't been in a very good mood.'

'Take him dancing,' he said. 'Or read him my most optimistic poem: "Le petit rondeau, le petit rondeau". That one was a real triumph. He'll want to know what "rondeau" means, so tell him it's the dance that's supplanted the Macarena.'

'I wish you liked each other,' I said, 'but realistically speaking, he has three siblings and the only one he talks to is his sister.'

'I could wear a wig. Everybody's getting chemo now, so they're making very convincing hair.'

We turned the corner. Snow was falling fast, and people hurried along. He wasn't wearing a hat or a scarf. What had I been thinking? In solidarity, I left my little knitted beret folded in my coat pocket.

'Let's go there,' he said, pointing to a Mexican restaurant. 'Who wants all those truffles and frills? A cold Dos Equis on a cold day, a beef burrito. That'll be fine.'

I could tell that walking was an effort. Also, I'd realized his shoes were surprisingly heavy as I put them on.

We went into the Mexican restaurant. Two doctors in scrubs were eating at one of the two front tables. An old lady and a young woman sat at another. We were shown to the back room, where a table of businessmen were laughing. I took off my coat and asked Franklin if he needed help with his. 'My leg won't bend,' he said. 'That's happened before. It locks. I can sit down, but I'm going to need an arm.'

'Seriously?'

'Yes.'

The waiter reached around us and put menus on the table and rushed away. I pulled out a chair. How was I going to get it near the table again, though? I was just about to push it a little closer to the table when Franklin made a hopping motion with one foot and stabilized himself by grabbing the edge of the table and bending at the waist. Before I knew it, he was sitting in the chair, wincing, one leg bent, the other extended. 'Go get those doctor fellows and tell 'em I swalled Viagra, and my leg's completely rigid,' he said. 'Tell 'em it's been this way for at least ten hours.'

I dropped a glove, and when I bent to pick it up I also tried to move the chair in closer to the table. I couldn't budge it. And the waiter looked smaller than I was.

'Let's see,' Franklin said, picking up one of the menus. 'Let's see if there's a simple bean burrito for a simple old guy, and our waiter can bring a brace of beer bottles by their necks and we can have a drink and make a toast to the knee that will bend, to Egil our friend, to a life without end . . . at least, let's hope it's not rigor mortis setting in at a Mexican restaurant.'

'Three Dos Equis, and you can serve one to my friend,' Franklin said to the waiter. 'Excuse me for sitting out in the middle of the room, but I like to be at the centre of the action.'

'You want me to maybe help you in a little closer to the table?' the waiter said, coming close to Franklin's side.

'Well, I don't know,' Franklin said doubtfully, but he slid forward a bit on the chair, and with one quick movement, he rose slightly, the waiter pushed the chair under him and he was suddenly seated a normal distance from the table.

'*Gracias, mi amigo,*' Franklin said.

'No problem,' the waiter said. He turned to me. 'You're going to have a Dos Equis?'

I spread my hands helplessly and smiled.

At that exact moment, my ex-husband and a very attractive woman walked into the back room, following a different waiter. He stopped and we stared at each other in disbelief. He and I had met at Penn, but for a long time now I'd lived in Charlottesville. Last time I'd heard, he was living in Santa Fe. He said something hurriedly to the pretty woman and, instead of sitting, pointed to a different table, in the corner. The waiter complied with the request, but only the woman walked away. My ex-husband came to our table.

'What a surprise,' Gordy said. 'Nice to see you.'

'Nice to see you,' I echoed.

'I'd rise, but I took Viagra and now I can't get my leg to move,' Franklin said. He had settled on this as the joke of the day.

'Professor Chadwick?' Gordy said. 'Franklin Chadwick, right? Gordon Miller. I was president of Latin Club.'

'That's right!' Franklin said. 'And back then, we were both in love with the same girl!'

Gordy blushed and took a step back. 'That's right. Good to see you. Sorry to interrupt.' He was not wearing a wedding ring. He turned and strode back toward the faraway table.

'Why did you say that?' I asked. 'You were never in love with me. You were always flirting with Louisa Kepper. You paid her to cut your grass so you could stare at her in shorts and work boots. She knew it, too.'

'I wasn't in love with you, but now it seems like I should have been, because where are they now? Who keeps in touch? I never hear, even when a poem is published. It was just a job, apparently. Like a bean burrito's a bean burrito.'

'Here you go, three beers. Should I pour for you?' the waiter asked.

'I'll take mine in the bottle,' Franklin said, reaching up. The waiter handed him the bottle.

'Yes, thank you,' I said. The waiter poured two-thirds of a glass of beer and set the bottle beside my glass. 'Lunch is coming,' he said.

'I'll tell you what I'd like: a shot of tequila on the side.'

'We only have a beer and wine licence. I'm sorry,' the waiter said.

'Then let me have a glass of red wine on the side,' Franklin said.

'OK,' the waiter said.

'Take it easy with the drinking. I've got to get you back in one piece,' I said. 'Also, I don't want to feel like an enabler. I want us to have a good time, but we can do that sober.'

'"Enabler"? Don't use phoney words like that. They're ugly, Maude.'

I was startled when he used my name. I'd been 'Champ' in his poetry seminar. We were all 'Champ'. The biggest champ had now published six books. I had published one, though it had won the Yale Series. We didn't talk about the fact that I'd stopped writing poetry.

'I hope you understand that he and I –' he tilted his head in the direction of my ex-husband – 'had a man-to-man on the telephone, and I told him where we'd be eating today.'

'I wonder what he *is* doing here. I thought he lived in Santa Fe.'

'Probably got tired of all the sun, and the turquoise and coyotes. Decided to trade it in for snow, and a grey business suit and squirrels.'

'Did you see if she had a wedding ring on?' I asked.

'Didn't notice. When I'm with one pretty girl, what do I care about another? Though there's that great story by Irwin Shaw, "The Girls in Their Summer Dresses". I don't suppose anyone even mentions Irwin Shaw any more. They might, if only he'd thought to call his story "The Amazingly Gorgeous Femme Fatales Provoke Envy and Lust as Men Go Mad".' He turned to the waiter, who'd appeared with the bean burrito and the chicken enchilada I'd ordered.

'Sir, will you find occasion to drop by that table in the corner and see if the lady is wearing a wedding ring?' Franklin said quietly into the waiter's ear.

'No problem,' the waiter said. He put down the plates. He lifted two little dishes of sauce from the tray and put them on the table. 'No joke, my brother José is the cook. I hope you like it. I'm getting your wine now.'

The first bite of enchilada was delicious. I asked Franklin if he'd like to taste it. He shook his head no. He waited until the waiter returned with the glass of wine, then took a big sip before lifting his burrito, or trying to. It was too big. He had to pick up a fork. He didn't use the knife to cut it, just the fork. I'd studied him for so long, almost nothing surprised me any more, however small the gesture. I had a fleeting thought that perhaps part of the reason I'd stopped writing was that I studied him, instead. But now I was also noticing little lapses, which made everything different for both of us. I liked the conversational quirks, not the variations or the repetitions. Two months ago, when I'd visited, bringing fried chicken and a bottle of his favourite white wine, Sancerre (expensive stuff), he'd told me about the receptionist, though that time he'd told me she'd had the surgery in Denmark.

The waiter came back and made his report: 'Not what I'd call a wedding ring. It's a dark stone, I think maybe amethyst, but I don't think it's a wedding ring, and she has gold rings on two other fingers, also.'

'We assume, then, she's just wearing rings.'

The waiter nodded. 'You want another glass of wine, just let me know.'

'He and I had a man-to-man last night and he promised to keep me supplied,' he said. 'I told you the guy with the Messerschmitt gets drug deliveries? Thugs that arrive together, like butch nuns on testosterone. Two, three in the morning. Black guys, dealers. They're all How-ya-doin'-man best friends with the receptionist. That's the night guy. Hispanic. Had a breakdown, lives with his brother. Used to work at Luxor in Vegas.'

'Take a bite of your burrito,' I said, and instantly felt like a mother talking to her child. The expression on his face told me he thought I was worse than that. He said nothing and finished his wine. There was a conspicuous silence.

'Everything good?' the waiter said. He'd just seated a table of three men, one of them choosing to keep on his wet coat. He sat at the table, red-nosed, looking miserable.

Leaning forward to look, I'd dropped my napkin. As I bent to pick it up, the waiter appeared, unfurling a fresh one like a magician who'd come out of nowhere. I half expected a white bird to fly up. But my mind was racing: there'd been a stain on Franklin's sock. Had he stepped in something on the way to the restaurant, or was it, as I feared, blood? I waited until the nice waiter wasn't looking and pushed back the tablecloth enough to peek. The stain was bright red, on the foot with the unfastened Velcro.

'Franklin, your foot,' I said. 'Does it hurt? I think your foot is bleeding.'

'My feet don't feel. That's the problem,' he said.

I pushed back my chair and inspected the foot more carefully. Yes, a large area of the white sock was bloody. I was really frightened.

'Eat your lunch,' he said. 'And I'll eat mine. Don't worry.'

'It might . . . it could be a problem. Has this ever happened before?'

He didn't answer. He was now using both his fork and knife to cut his burrito.

'Maybe I could run to CVS and find some bandages. That's what I'll do.'

But I didn't move. I'd seen a drugstore walking to the restaurant, but where? I could ask the waiter. I'd ask the waiter and hope he didn't know why I was asking. He might want to be too helpful, he might insist on walking us to a cab, I might not get to eat my lunch, though the thought of taking another bite revolted me now. I'd wanted to say something meaningful, have what people think of as *a lovely lunch*. Were we going to end up at the hospital? Wasn't that what we were going to have to do? There was a fair amount of blood. I got up, sure that I had to do something, but what? Wouldn't it be sensible to call his doctor?

'Everything OK?' the waiter said. I found that I was standing in the centre of the room, looking over my shoulder toward the table where Franklin was eating his lunch.

'Fine, thank you. Is there a drugstore nearby?'

'Right across the street,' he said. 'Half a block down.'

'Good. OK, I'm going to run to the drugstore,' I said, 'but maybe you shouldn't bring him anything else to drink until –' and then I fainted. When my eyes opened, my ex-husband was holding my hand, and the pretty woman was gazing over his shoulder, as the waiter fanned me with a menu. The man in the wet wool coat was saying my name – everyone must have heard it when Franklin yelped in surprise, though he couldn't rise, he saw it with his eyes, my toppling was unwise . . .

'Hey, Maude, hey hey, Maude,' Wet Coat was saying. 'OK, Maude, you with us? Maude, Maude? You're OK, open your eyes if you can. Can you hear me, Maude?'

Franklin, somehow, was standing. He shimmered in my peripheral vision. There was blood on the rug. I saw it but couldn't speak. I had a headache and the thrumming made a pain rhyme: He couldn't rise / He saw it with his eyes. And it was so odd, so truly odd that my ex-husband was holding my hand again, after one hundred years away, in the castle of Luxor. It all ran together. I was conscious, but I couldn't move.

'We had sex under the table, which you were kind enough to pretend not to observe, and she's got her period,' Franklin said. I heard him say it distinctly, as if he were spitting out the words. And I saw that the waiter was for the first time flummoxed. He looked at me as if I could give him a clue, but damn it, all I was managing to whisper was 'OK', and I wasn't getting off the floor.

'The colour's coming back to your face,' my husband said. 'What happened? Do you know?'

'Too much sun and turquoise,' I said, and though at first he looked very puzzled, he got my drift, until he lightened his grip on my wrist, then began lightly knocking his thumb against it, as if sending Morse code: tap, tap-tap, tap. He and the pretty woman stayed with me even after I could stand, after the waiter took me into his brother's office and helped them get me into an armchair. For some reason, the cook gave me his business card and asked for mine. My ex-husband got one out of a little envelope in my wallet and handed it to him, obviously thinking it was as strange a request as I did. 'She didn't have nothing to drink, one sip of beer,' the waiter said, defending me. 'She saw blood, I don't know, sometimes the ladies faint at the sight of blood.'

'He's such a crude old coot,' my ex-husband said. 'I should be impressed with your loyalty, but I never knew what you saw in him.'

Savannah the receptionist came for Franklin, and he went to the hospital – but not before paying the bill from a wad of money I didn't know he was carrying, and not before taking a Mexican hat off the wall, insisting that he was 'just borrowing it, like an umbrella'.

'There might be an Indian uprising if we stop him,' the waiter's brother said to him. 'Let him go.' He called out to Franklin, 'Hey, pard, you keep that hat and wear it if they storm the Alamo.'

I thought about that, and thought about it, and finally thought José hadn't really meant anything by it, that a little shoplifting was easy to deal with, especially when the culprit announced what he was doing.

With the worried transgendered woman beside him, and Franklin holding her arm, it was amazing that he could shuffle in a way that allowed him to bend enough to kiss my cheek. 'Awake, Princess,' he said, 'and thank God our minions were all too smart to call an ambulance.'

He refused dialysis and died at the end of April, which, for him, certainly was the cruellest month. I spoke to him the day after I fainted in the restaurant, and he told me they'd put leeches on his foot; the second time, several weeks later, he was worried that it might have to be amputated. 'You're the ugly stepsister who crammed my foot into the slipper,' he said. 'And time's the ugly villain that made me old. I was a proper shit-kicker in my Luccheses. I would have had you under the table back in the day. But you're right, I never loved you. Maybe you'll find something to write about when I'm dead, because you sure aren't kicking your own shit while I'm still alive.'

If you can believe it, that Christmas I got a card from the Mexican restaurant, signed by staff I'd never even met. It could have been a crib sheet for remembering that painful day: a silver Christmas tree with glitter that came off on my fingertips and some cute little animals clustered at the base, wearing caps with pompoms and tiny scarves. A squirrel joined them, standing on its haunches, holding sheet music, as Santa streaked overhead, Rudolph leading the way. Rudolph. What had become of Rudolph?

There was no memorial service that I heard of, though a few people called or wrote me when they saw the obituary. 'Was he still full of what he called "piss and vinegar" up to the end? You kept in touch with him, didn't you?' Carole Kramer (who'd become a lawyer in New York) wrote me. I wrote her back that he'd had to give up his cowboy boots, but I could assure her he was still full of piss and vinegar, and didn't say that it was an inability to piss that finally killed him, and that he'd drunk himself to death, wine, vinegar, it didn't really matter.

He'd mentioned squirrels the last day I'd seen him, though, so now when I saw them I paid more attention, even if everyone in Washington thought of them as rats with bushy tails. I even bought one a roasted chestnut on a day I was feeling sentimental, but the squirrel dropped it like it was poison, and I could see from the gleam in the eye of the guy cooking the nuts that he was glad I'd gotten my comeuppance.

Then winter ended and spring came, and I thought, even if I don't believe there's a poem in anything any more, maybe I'll write a story. A lot of people do that when they can't seem to figure out who or what they love. It might be an oversimplification, but they seem to write poetry when they do know. ■

THE DEFEATED

Jonny Steinberg

1.

In October 1999, in the KwaZulu-Natal province of South Africa, a young man I've named Peter Mitchell was shot to death on his father's farm at about two o'clock on a Monday afternoon. He was twenty-eight years old, a big, chunky guy, square-faced and blond. In his graduation pictures, he towers above his parents, the three of them awfully grim-faced and serious, as if decorum required them to drain their faces of pride. I have long ago given up wondering what sort of person he was. Four or five pen sketches of him fill my old notebooks, each placing him in a different story, playing a different role. The thing about the dead, especially when they die the way Peter did, is that nobody speaks honestly about them.

Beyond question, though, was the identity of the killers.

He was on his way to tend his father's cabbages when he died, a routine journey travelled day in and day out. He was driving his father's jeep along a dirt road cut from dense bush. It was the perfect road for a nasty surprise.

The killers would not have known in advance whom they were going to shoot. Father and son took turns to tend the cabbages. It did not matter, really; either would do.

They chose a shotgun for the job, the lip of its barrel no more than a metre or so away when the bullet slammed into the flesh behind Peter's left ear. From the entry wound, it appeared that he was looking to his right when he died. Somebody on the right-hand side of the road must have hailed him. Directly on his left, up against the road, was a tall, thick bush, a deep hollow just behind it. The assassin could have stood there at full height, entirely unseen.

The killers took his 9mm pistol, but they did not bother with his cellphone or his wallet; there was no attempt to feign a robbery. They wanted the old man to know that they'd gotten his son.

The Mitchells were new; they had come recently from the city. Farming was for them an exciting adventure, an opportunity to toss caution to the wind and try something different. Nine months earlier, they had bought three adjacent farms strung out across the slopes of a remote valley. There was Eleanor, where they lived and ran cattle; Derbytin, where they irrigated cabbages and tomatoes; and, wedged between the other two farms, Normandale, the property on which Peter died.

In a corner of Normandale, up against the district road, was a fenced-off piece of land, one hundred hectares in all, called Langeni. On it lived nine Zulu families, all of them dirt poor, without running water or electricity, but with a lot of history. The oldest of them had lived on that ground for five generations, serving the successive white masters of Normandale, the first of whom was Isaiah Player, who acquired the land in 1911. It passed to his son, John, who sold it to Mr Laurie Steyn in 1969, who ran it for twenty-seven years until his retirement in March 1996. Steyn struggled to find a new buyer, and the farm stood without a white proprietor for three years until February 1999, when the new man from the city, Arthur Mitchell, acquired it, his big, blond son always at his side.

Mitchell's purchase of Normandale was no small matter for the nine families. In that part of the world, the temperament of the white man with the title deed had always counted a great deal, for the rules governing your relationship with him were not written down and much was at stake.

Your landlord allowed you to live on his land, to use a small portion of it to grow maize and vegetables and to graze cattle. He allowed you to raise your family there. Customarily, he and his neighbours would build a little farm school in which your children could complete their first three or four years of schooling. If somebody fell gravely ill, you got a child to run to the big house and the farmer would take the sick one to the doctor.

In exchange, he asked for your family's labour: yours, your wife's, your children's. That was the deal.

True, each district had its customs, its set of unwritten rules. If your employer breached what was considered reasonable, there were ways of making his life hard. But still, the white man's judgement counted a great deal. He could, for instance, until recent times, pull your kid out of school to work on the farm. He could restrict the number of cattle you could graze to a minimum and thus deplete your family of its assets and its wealth. For the relationship to work, something human had to pass between you and the white man, something generous.

When apartheid ended in 1994, some two million black South African labour tenants were living under the proprietorship of 50,000 or so white farmers. What was to become of their relationship now that apartheid was over? For everyone to cast ballots in the same election, each vote counting as much as the next, and then to return home to a world of conqueror and conquered – the dissonance was too jarring. The Mitchells were new, but they had stepped into the drama of an endgame.

When Arthur Mitchell bought Normandale in 1999 he went down to Langeni with his son Peter to meet his tenants. His Zulu was not very good and his tenants spoke barely any English at all. He brought with him as a translator a young constable from the local police station. Whether he understood this as a provocation, I am not sure.

He assembled his tenants on the side of the district road and told them that Normandale would be out of bounds for them. The one hundred hectares of Langeni was theirs. The rest was his. They were not to graze their cattle on Normandale, they were not to collect firewood there, they were not to cross the land when they drew water from the river.

If a tenant wanted to build an extension to his home, he was to ask Mitchell's permission. If a daughter has had a child, he said, and the young family needs some privacy, that is a good reason to build a new hut. But if it is to bring new people onto the property, Mitchell would forbid it.

Which brought him to his third rule. He wanted a list of the names and identity numbers of every person who lived on the property. If he found a person who did not belong, he would evict that person.

A middle-aged man named Mhila Mashabana, a member of one of the oldest Langeni families, interrupted Mitchell.

'We do not give our names to white people,' he said. 'We do not trust what you will do with them.'

The way Mitchell remembers it, Mashabana was very aggressive. He spoke as if issuing a dare. He wanted to up the temperature, to make Mitchell shout.

'I would not do that,' Mitchell recalled later. Instead, he ended the meeting immediately. He and Peter went back to the farmhouse at Eleanor, and the young police constable went back to the police station.

One night the following week, a cottage on Eleanor burnt to the ground. Mitchell went to the police station and laid a charge of arson against Mashabana.

The following week, on a routine drive across his farms, Mitchell came across three head of cattle. They belonged to the Cube family, one of the original Langeni tenants. He had the cattle impounded and carted off to the nearest state-run holding centre, more than sixty kilometres away. To get them back, the Cubes would have to pay a hefty fine and transport costs, a great deal more than they could afford.

The following night, fences all over the Mitchell properties went down. Usually, when people destroyed fences, it was to use the wire and the poles in their own yards. But in these instances, the fences were simply left where they fell, flat on the ground.

By September, Mitchell's tenants had torn down every last fence post on his properties and burnt several fields. The Mitchell farms were strewn with the debris of war and the filing cabinet at the local police station was thick with records of accusation.

Mitchell called another meeting. He brought the same young police constable with him. And he brought Peter. Once more, the tenants assembled at the side of the district road.

Mitchell started from the beginning. He spoke of the building rule and of the collection of names. He said, too, that each family was restricted to keeping five head of cattle.

Mashabana rose once more and said that he did not accept Mitchell's rules. He would keep as many cattle as he pleased. From the Cube family came murmurs of encouragement. There and then, through the police interpreter, Mitchell told Mashabana to pack his bags and leave. If he remained any longer on this land where he had been born, Mitchell told him, he would be trespassing.

Mashabana turned and walked away while the others remained grim and silent. Three weeks later, the young blond man who had witnessed these scenes at his father's side was dead.

I met Arthur Mitchell a couple of months after Peter died. He was hitting sixty, a short man with a belly and that sort of pale, milky skin that blisters red in the sun. We sat in his living room drinking tea. His manner of speaking was like his face in his son's graduation picture, the emotion all washed out. Whenever he spoke, it sounded as if he were reciting a list.

I took notes while we talked. His home seemed austere and generic, I wrote, more an emblem of a middle-class home than a particular family's abode. I noted that his wife had absented herself for my visit, and that there were no pictures of his son, not in the public parts of his home. The two of us alone in this house, just the sound of his soft, toneless voice and my murmurs of acknowledgement – it seemed an awfully empty place.

The day after Peter died, Arthur Mitchell drove his jeep along his rutted road, past the murder scene, to his fields. He assembled the women who picked his cabbages and named his bounty.

'Every one of you knows who killed my son,' he said in broken Zulu. 'I will pay thirty thousand rand to the person who produces good information.' Thirty thousand was perhaps three times more than the women would have earned had they picked his cabbages all year round.

And then he went back to work. Each morning, he would drive past the site of his son's murder to see to his cabbages. And each afternoon he drove back. One night, an old black man knocked on his door and told him that the Cubes were planning to kill him on his dirt track, just as they had killed his son.

Mitchell duly informed the police, but that offered little protection. They had been questioning people in Langeni incessantly and had come up with nothing. They were hardly going to prevent another murder.

And so, on his daily journey to his cabbage fields, he began to take with him his Alsatian, Fletcher, a pump-action shotgun, a 9mm pistol, and two brown-skinned mercenaries who had once fought for the apartheid government's army, each armed with an automatic weapon. He'd be damned, he said, if they'd chase him from his farm.

'If one of them appeared on my front lawn,' he told me in that even voice of his, 'I would be absolutely delighted; I could blow him to pieces within the four corners of the law.'

His wife, neighbouring farmers confided to me, was beside herself. All she wanted to do was leave. She had daughters in Australia. She could take comfort in her remaining children and never see this farm again. But he would not go. He armed himself to the teeth every morning, to farm. He was choosing death over life.

It was the darkness inside him that allowed me into his story. He could not blow his son's killers to pieces. And the police had arrested nobody. When I came along he saw an opportunity. He would expose a little of himself to me and I would expose his enemy to the world. 'I have done no wrong,' he told me several times, 'so even if you are working for the CIA, I have nothing to worry about.'

He had a lot to worry about. To climb out of the ditch of vengeance into which he had fallen, to gain enough height to see the tale I was bound to tell, was an imaginative journey he could not take. These notes I jotted down – about his living room, his shotgun, about the absence of his wife – were to be enlisted into the story of his terrible relationship with his tenants. However carefully I might write, however alive I might be to historical forces beyond his control, the fact remains that in putting Arthur Mitchell on the page I was asking whether he was responsible for his son's death.

Peter Mitchell died on a frontier, not so much between black and white, or between the landed and the landless, as between the past and the future. South African democracy was a little over five years old on the day he was killed. White people did not die that way under apartheid. To shoot one's landlord's son and return to one's huts; to go on as if nothing had happened, the white man now tending his vegetables with an army in tow – power was ebbing from its old strongholds.

Peter was a casualty of an unheralded in-between time, a battle, never named or commemorated, over what would replace the age-old relationship between white landlord and black labour tenant.

In the mid-1990s, South Africa's new democratically elected parliament passed several statutes that offered black people on white-owned farmland security of tenure. In response, many white farmers began destroying the fixed structures on their land.

'When an old man dies,' the owner of a large commercial farm about fifty kilometres from Normandale told me, 'we bust up his house so that nobody else can move in. His children must live elsewhere. If they make a claim on the land, we go to court to contest it and we usually win because we can work the law better than they can. A generation from now, there will be no black people on the land. We are mechanizing. What labour we need we will employ by the day; it is easy to recruit from the slums.'

In the last decade of the twentieth century, almost a million black

South Africans left their homes on white-owned land. They filled up the rural slums and shacklands from which farmers now recruited their labour.

If that was a typical white strategy in the face of the new, what was a typical black strategy? To express displeasure at a new landlord's rules by burning his cottage and his fields? Was that how one signalled that things had changed? And if he did not learn fast, did you then take out his son?

Mitchell had a theory about his son's murder. The head of the local branch of the African National Congress, South Africa's former liberation movement and now its ruling party, was a man called Paul Mlambo.

'Paul told the black families in the valley,' Mitchell said to me, 'if you can force each white farmer in that valley off his land, it will all be yours.'

'How do you know that he said this?' I asked.

'I have my sources,' he replied.

I was wary of the language Mitchell used when he discussed these matters. He spoke of the communist mentality, of secret cells and of the power of terror tactics.

'Take out the strongest white farmer and the rest will flee,' he said. 'That is the logic of terror. It is very effective. That is why I will not leave. I am stronger than that.'

In Mitchell's understanding, Laurie Steyn, the man from whom he'd bought Normandale, had been forced off his land by the Cubes and the Mashabanas. This seemed a fair assessment to me. When I went to see Steyn he told me that his relationship with his tenants had run swimmingly, but the stories he told made my hair stand on end. He believed that his tenants were all thieves. He would pay the Mashabanas to tell him what the Cubes were stashing in their huts and he would pay the Cubes to inform him what the Mashabanas were stashing. Periodically, he raided both families' homes in the middle of the night, turning everyone out of their beds and rifling through their possessions.

In return, his fields were set alight and his cattle slaughtered. During the last few years, things got rougher. A white man who lived in a caravan on the Steyn property was shot between the ribs one night while watching television. Miraculously, the bullet missed all vital organs and he recovered. On an evening some months later, Steyn heard strange noises around his house and when he went outside to investigate he was greeted by a volley of shots.

'Either they were merely trying to frighten me,' he said, 'or their aim is as useless as everything else they try to do.'

Mitchell bought Normandale because it was wedged between his vegetable farm and his cattle farm and it was no longer controlled by a white proprietor. He told me that he bought the place in order to keep the tenants confined to Langeni and to prevent new black families from moving onto the land.

'If they and their people are free to roam all over Normandale, farming will become impossible for me,' he said. 'Their cattle will mix with mine and bring diseases. The land will soon be teeming with strangers come to live here; they will break the fences and steal from me. I cannot afford to have a squatter camp on my doorstep.'

But my guess is that he wanted to push the tenants off the land. Other farmers in neighbouring districts had done it. They established rules of occupation that made their tenants' lives unliveable and they watched like hawks until a tenant committed a crime. Then they would go to court, and evict.

Getting the other side of the story was nearly impossible at first. The murder was fresh and unsolved and I was a white stranger without credentials. Nobody at Langeni had any reason to talk to me.

And then something happened.

From the start, the South African Police Service's handling of the feud between the Mitchells and their tenants had divided along racial lines. The Cubes and the Mashabanas used the black detectives from the local police station. Mitchell used a specialized murder investigation unit run by white people.

Several months after the murder, somebody among the Langeni tenants with an eye on Mitchell's 30,000-rand bounty whispered a story into a neighbouring white farmer's ear.

Late one night in May 2000, a carload of white detectives swooped upon Langeni and pulled a young man from his bed. He was twenty years old and his name was Bheki Cube. The police had been told that he had buried a shotgun and a pistol somewhere on the property. They gave him a spade and ordered him to dig. The two of them took him off into the darkness. About ten minutes passed, and then the people of Langeni heard several shots.

Young Cube had finally found the pistol, the detectives said. He had cocked it and pointed it at them and they had killed him in self-defence.

The following morning, Mitchell went to his cabbage fields. The harvesting season was drawing to a close. About two dozen casual labourers, some of them women from Langeni, were in the fields. He instructed them to stop working and gather around him.

'The Cubes took my son,' he told them. 'And now the Good Lord has taken one of theirs.'

On the day of Bheki Cube's funeral, I employed an elderly Zulu man to walk into the Cube home to offer his condolences. He was in his late sixties and had grown up in those parts. He told the Cubes that he had heard of the death of their son and had travelled from his home in Pietermaritzburg to pay his respects. He was a retired policeman, he explained, and when he heard stories about police killing young men, like in the old days, it upset him. He spent several hours with the Cubes and left with their account of their relationship with Mitchell.

'He was trying to force them off the land,' the old man told me. 'If they cannot collect firewood from Normandale, they have no means to light their stoves. If they cannot walk through his land to the river, they have no access to water. They have been on that land five generations. They have nowhere else to go.'

'What did you make of the Cubes?' I asked the old man. 'Were they good people? Bad people?'

'Just people,' he replied. 'Ordinary folk.'

'They gunned down a young man in cold blood,' I said. 'Do ordinary folk do that?'

I had been working with the old man for several months and had grown to like him very much. He had a gentle way about him; he was gracious and kind. But now he looked at me coldly, with the unpleasant, estranged look a black person sometimes gives a white person.

'If I had been living there five generations,' he said, 'and a new landlord told me in broken Zulu that he wanted to interview my family before I could build a hut on my own land, I would also have killed him.'

2.

Fourteen years after Peter Mitchell's murder, I was eating breakfast at a resort on South Africa's eastern seaboard when the proprietors of the place, a husband and wife, asked if they could join me at my table.

The woman introduced herself as Wendy. She had seen my name in the guestbook, she said, and she wanted me to know that her parents had farmed in the same valley as the Mitchells. She had grown up there, just a couple of kilometres down the road.

I had published a book on the Mitchell killing eleven years earlier. It had sold well and got attention. When it won a prestigious prize, several farmers in the district co-signed a letter published in the local newspaper saying that the book ought to have been awarded the Lenin Prize. I was *persona non grata* among them, I was told.

Arthur Mitchell had read a draft of the manuscript several months before publication; he told me that he found it troubling but OK. His equanimity did not last after publication. The local newspaper carried extracts on three successive days and the whole district was talking about it. By the end of the week, Mitchell was enraged.

'Your description of my furniture,' he said. 'And the absence of Peter's pictures. How dare you.'

Only once his neighbours had seen these things did he understand the betrayal. It was as if all their homes had been flung open to the eyes of strangers, as if all their relationships with black tenants had been held up for scrutiny. Until the day his neighbours read the extracts, he thought it was only his own privacy he'd been trading.

Our last meeting was tense and unhappy. In farewell, he handed me a copy of the picture taken at Peter's graduation ceremony. We have not communicated since.

Now here was Wendy, the first white resident of that district I had encountered in eleven years. She was my age, more or less: early forties. While she spoke, her husband looked on with interest and her dog, an English Pointer, rested his chin on her lap.

'I think you should know,' she said, 'that my generation has gone back to the district to farm. We went off to university. We travelled. And then, one by one, the people I went to school with returned. My sister and her husband are there. Many others, too. They are not like the older generation. They are more forward-looking, more progressive. The district is peaceful now. There is no trouble there.'

I was leaving that morning and we did not talk more. But Wendy stuck in my mind and I phoned her sometime later and asked for her sister's contact details. The sister's name was Mel and she was as friendly and welcoming as Wendy. The following month, I found myself driving back into that valley for the first time in more than a decade. For the occasion of my visit, Mel had invited about a dozen white farmers around for lunch – all of them, she said, eager to meet me. I was to stay over for the night with her and her husband.

I was the last to arrive. Several men and women were standing on a patio drinking beer. Young kids were running around the garden. There were salad platters and bowls of vegetables. Four chickens roasted on a barbecue outside.

We assembled around a large dining-room table and the conversation was like so many middle-class conversations – it could really have taken place anywhere. A recent holiday to Thailand where the tour guide was as camp as you can imagine and introduced himself as Saucy Martin. A discussion about stem-cell therapy for cancer and another about getting quality teachers to come and work in so remote a district. The talk turned to land and farming and crime, but the spirit remained the same – it was all lightness and merriment.

'The Farm Watch closed down a couple of years after you were here,' I was told. 'It was really something for the older generation – patrolling the land with guns.'

'What do you do about security?' I asked.

A shrug. 'We're meant to patrol around Christmas time, but usually we forget.'

'There's no crime here any more?' I asked, a little incredulous.

In fact, I was told, a local farmer, a man they all knew well, had been murdered in his home two months earlier. It was the first killing of a white farmer since Peter Mitchell.

'It was terrible,' a farmer called Hilton said. 'But it didn't create the drama Peter's murder created. We didn't think the world was ending. We didn't think they were chasing us off the land. After the murder, an expert on rural crime came to talk to us. He said, "Guys, statistically, a farmer is going to get murdered once every seven years in every farm district in this country. That's how it is. One of you takes it for the team, the rest get on with it."'

I asked after Arthur Mitchell.

'He and his wife live in Perth,' I was told. 'With their daughters.'

'How are they?' I asked.

A long silence.

'Nobody here has been in touch with them for years.'

The silence continued another moment or two, the distance between these people and Arthur Mitchell filling the room.

'Who farms there now?' I asked.

'Nobody. His tenants claimed it. It is held on their behalf by the Department of Land Affairs. But they are too poor to farm it. And Land Affairs can't get it together to give them capital or train them. Normandale just stands there. Unused.'

M el's husband, John, had grown up in the district, not far from Normandale. As a young man he'd gone away and studied, then spent a few years in Europe. He came back shortly after Peter's death and began farming. That evening, after the guests were gone, I asked him why he thought Peter Mitchell had been killed.

'You were correct to make Arthur and the previous owner, Laurie Steyn, the protagonists,' he replied. 'They were too military-minded, too aggressive. And the tragedy is that they brought on Peter's death. I find that hard to handle. He was such a gentle guy. He had nothing to do with any of that stuff. He didn't care about black and white.'

'Laurie wanted –'

'I have to admit,' he interrupted, 'I thought like them back then. When Laurie said we must stock up with guns because they were going to take our land, I believed him. I was very frightened. It is embarrassing to admit it now, but I wanted to fight. We had all spent some time in the army; it is very powerful, the indoctrination there. You have to remember those times. There was a lot of violence down in that valley. We were very unsure what was going to happen next. We were thinking that they were taking us out one by one in order to get that land. Looking back now I feel foolish, but that is how I felt then.'

'You say that Arthur brought on Peter's murder,' I said, 'but it wouldn't have been an easy situation for anybody. The Cubes do not seem like nice people. They may have taken on anyone who bought that land.'

He shook his head. 'Black people made a claim on my land under the new legislation in 1998,' he said. 'I was in such a state. I was literally in tears. In retrospect, I should not have lost a second's sleep. The claim came to nothing in the end, but even if they had taken a big chunk of my farm, so what? As long as they compensate me for it, they can take what they like. There are many ways to turn a buck here. The golden rule is not to be sentimental. Forget the Jack Russell buried under the tree. This is just a business. No more. To roll up your sleeves and fight them the way Arthur did. What for?'

He said goodnight and left me with a pile of documents about the claims on his land and as I sat there alone I absorbed the distaste these young white farmers felt for Arthur Mitchell and it left me uncomfortable. Mitchell's memory was an embarrassment to them now, a reminder of a time when they were fearful and did stupid things.

'We are too clever to be killed by our labourers,' I hear them say to themselves. 'We are too adaptable. Too light on our feet.'

It has taken time, but they have learned. The earth beneath their feet does not belong to them. They step lightly upon it. Their weapons are their smarts, their sophistication. With these, they can make money. And when it is time to leave, they will up and go.

Yet it was Mitchell and his generation who made this new sophistication possible. It was their paranoia and their racism and their violence. They were the ones who did the dirty work; they pushed close to a million South Africans from their ancestral land. They extricated their own children from the poisoned relationship between white landlord and black tenant. The Johns of this world can tread lightly now because the battles of their fathers are over and things have settled.

The dining room where we had eaten lunch looked out over the valley in which the Mitchells once farmed. I'd kept gazing at it.

There had been nine white farmers in the valley on the day Peter Mitchell was killed.

'Why have they all left?' I asked.

They shrugged, said they weren't sure. The soil was not good there. It wasn't easy to irrigate. So many people tried and failed.

Perhaps Peter Mitchell's death had handed his neighbours a lesson. If the tenants in that valley were prepared to kill for the land, let them have it. Sell it to the government at a market rate and buy land a mile away, or ten miles away, where there were no more tenants.

The Cubes had no landlord now. They had won the most pyrrhic of victories.

The patriarch of the Cube family is a man named Mduduzi, but around the district he is referred to simply as Baba Cube, Father Cube, a designation of seniority and respect. He was arrested for Peter Mitchell's murder back in 2000, shortly before the police came to his homestead and killed his son, and spent several weeks in prison. He knew that there wasn't a shred of evidence against him and admitted to nothing.

'He was the hardest motherfucker I've ever encountered,' the white detective who interrogated him told me at the time. 'He never moved an inch.'

Now, all these years later, I went to Langeni and found him outside a shack called the Tea Room, one of those derelict country stores with near-empty shelves and groups of men and women sitting idly around the front door. Baba Cube was in late middle age. He had a bright silver beard and a head of uncombed silver hair and he was wiry and scrawny and demonstrably poor; the black T-shirt he wore faded and shapeless, his trousers unwashed and his feet bare.

I had brought with me an interpreter. He was, of all people, the mayor of Ixopo, the municipal district into which Langeni fell. I had met him at the side of the district road some fifteen kilometres back and he had instructed his driver and his bodyguard to take his car back to town and had gotten into my passenger seat. His name was David Nxumalo. He was my age, almost to the day, and he was a labour tenant's son. He had, in fact, grown up a stone's throw from Normandale on Wendy's parents' farm.

At the Tea Room, Nxumalo went to Baba Cube and told him what I wanted. Baba Cube got up slowly and came to sit in the back seat of my car. And so there we were, the chronicler of the Mitchell murder, the erstwhile primary suspect and a labour tenant turned successful politician.

Baba Cube said that his father and his grandfather had been born on Normandale, but that his great-grandfather had not.

'Where was he born?' I asked.

He pointed to a hill just a few hundred yards away.

'There was a dam on that hill,' he said. 'When my great-grandfather's nephew was little, he drowned in that dam. And so Mr Isaiah Player told the black people that we could not live there any more. He took us down to Langeni and cut us a hundred hectares of land and told us it was ours.'

'And before your great-grandfather?' I asked. 'How did your people come to be on this land?'

He shook his head. 'Nobody ever spoke to me about that,' he said.

For the following three hours, he told his story, a string of minutely remembered incidents strung across the length of a century, each about a white landlord, and what he had and had not done. All of Normandale's landlords had been cruel, he said. Mr Player had paid wages in kind, not in money, and so the family could buy nothing. They built their home from the clay in the river and they paid for the tin roof with their children's labour.

Mr Steyn was better, Baba Cube said. He paid some of the wages in money. But when he bought Normandale in 1969 he pulled Baba Cube out of school to work on the farm. Had the Cubes resisted, Baba Cube said, Steyn would have evicted them.

'I do not read and write,' Baba Cube said. 'It is the twenty-first century. What can you do in this century if you cannot read and write?'

But the worst landlord of all was the last, Mr Mitchell.

'His aim was to chase us away,' Baba Cube said. 'To abide by his rules was to have no water, no firewood, to watch your cattle being taken off to the pound. He wanted us gone.'

'Is that why his son was killed?' I asked.

'Mr Mitchell's police killed my son,' he replied. 'He thought that I killed his son, so his police came and killed my child.'

'Who did kill Mr Mitchell's son?' I asked.

'I know nothing about that,' he said.

David Nxumalo had grown uncomfortable. He was shifting irritably in his seat. It was not the talk of who murdered whom that bothered him. It was the fact that we would be leaving soon and that he had brought nothing for Baba Cube.

'These people are so horribly poor,' he said to me. 'To leave them empty-handed . . .' He took a wad of hundred-rand notes from his pocket and gave them to Baba Cube who nodded grimly and held the notes at his side. I also gave Baba Cube some money and took two enormous cabbages and a pumpkin and a bag of oranges from my boot and left them on the side of the road. They were a gift from Isaiah Player's grandson, ironically enough; I had visited him earlier in the day.

On the trip back to Ixopo, David Nxumalo was quiet, holding his body very still. I was thinking of Baba Cube. He had spent hours describing South African history as the story of three white men, as if everything that had happened over a hundred years was their doing.

'Three decades ago,' I said to David Nxumalo, 'your family and the Cubes were the same. You were labour tenants. You lived in the same valley. Now you are the mayor and they have nothing. What accounts for the difference?'

He smiled at me with an open face. I had known him for a little more than an afternoon but I knew already that he was a man with a good soul.

'Where did you meet Wendy?' he asked, in return.

I told him about the resort, and the breakfast.

'If you speak to Wendy again,' he said, his smile broadening, 'tell her I send my fondest regards. I knew her well when I was a child. We swam together in a dam on the farm: me, Wendy, her sister Mel and my siblings. Wendy and I – we liked each other very much.'

He was chuckling to himself now, his head filled with memories. Then he fell silent.

We were approaching town when he spoke again.

'I think that I have started answering your question,' he said. 'Wendy's father was a good man. He allowed my father's herd of cattle to grow. He encouraged it, in fact. He extended interest-free credit when we needed to buy something big. My father was able to send me to a good school.'

David's daughter came running out to greet him, a six- or seven-year-old girl. He held her hand as they walked together up the driveway of their handsome suburban home, and I wondered, as I watched them, whether the story he told was not too simple. Could it be that a family's trajectory, extending forever into the future, could rest entirely on the character of the white man who once employed them? There are always so many gaps in the stories people tell.

At that Sunday lunch with the farmers, somebody mentioned in passing, as if it had happened somewhere far away, that another white man had been murdered outside Langeni. How long ago? Nobody could really remember. Four years back, perhaps. What was his name? Jake? John? James? The conversation turned and the matter was not mentioned again.

His name was James Davies and he was thirty-two years old on the day he died. He worked for a wealthy Durban businessman who had bought up a vast swathe of land, several thousand acres in all. The idea was to build a game lodge and bring in lions and cheetahs and elephants and buffalo and to charge tourists a lot of money to experience the wild.

James Davies had been employed to manage the new game farm's ring fence, a huge job, for the boundary went on for miles and miles. It bordered a black settlement opposite Langeni for a few hundred yards, before swinging away to the north. The people living there objected to the fence. It separated them from the land they wanted to claim.

James received a call one morning from a team of workers erecting the fence by Langeni. There was a problem, he was told. He must come.

The workers were sitting down eating lunch when he arrived. One of them pulled out a pistol and shot James in the hip. He fled into the bush and collapsed several paces away, then got to his knees and put his hands in front of his face. His killer shot him between the eyes.

The murderer was a kid, twenty years old, the son of a labour tenant. In court, he said he had decided off his own bat to kill the white man, that there were no co-conspirators.

James Davies and his employer had wandered into the district from afar. They were not farmers. They did not have farmers' memories or farmers' smarts. Nobody told them what was obvious to everybody else – that one ought to keep a healthy distance from the defeated. ∎

AUTHOR'S NOTE: *I have used pseudonyms for the farmers, their tenants and their farms.*

PRAIRIE SCHOONER

BOOK PRIZE SERIES

2012 WINNERS

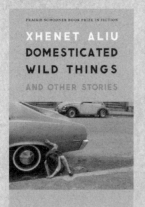

PRIZES $3,000 and publication through the University of Nebraska Press for one book of short fiction and one book of poetry.

ELIGIBILITY The Prairie Schooner Book Prize Series welcomes manuscripts from all writers, including non-U.S. citizens writing in English, and those who have previously published volumes of short fiction and poetry. No past or present paid employee of Prairie Schooner or the University of Nebraska Press or current faculty or students at the University of Nebraska will be eligible for the prizes.

JUDGING Semi-finalists will be chosen by members of the Prairie Schooner Book Prize Series National Advisory Board. Final manuscripts will be chosen by the Editor-in-Chief, **Kwame Dawes**.

HOW TO SEND We accept electronic submissions alongside hard copy submissions.

WHEN TO SEND Submissions will be accepted between **January 15** and **March 15, 2014**.

▪ **For submission guidelines or to submit online, visit prairieschooner.unl.edu.**

THE MAGIC BOX

Olivia Laing

DAVID WOJNAROWICZ
Arthur Rimbaud in New York (Times Square)
1978–79/2004
© P·P·O·W Gallery, New York

It never gets dark in Times Square. Sometimes I'd wake at two or three or four and watch waves of neon pass through my room. During these unwanted apertures of the night, I'd get out of bed and yank the useless curtain open. Outside, there was a Jumbotron, a giant electronic screen cycling perpetually through six or seven ads. One had gunfire, and one expelled a cold blue pulse of light, insistent as a metronome. Sometimes I'd count windows and sometimes I'd count buildings, though I never reached the end of either.

My room was on the corner of West 43rd Street and 8th Avenue, on the tenth floor of what had once been the Times Square Hotel. If I looked south, I could see the mirrored windows of the Westin. The gym was at eye level, and at odd hours I'd sometimes catch a figure churning circles on an exercise bike. The other window looked down onto a run of camera stores, bodegas, peep shows and lap-dancing clubs. It was a paradise of artificial light, in which the older technologies, the neon extravagances in the shape of whiskey glasses and dancing girls, were in the process of being made obsolete by the unremitting perfection of light-emitting diodes and liquid crystals.

I'd found the apartment the way I always did: by putting a plea on Facebook. It belonged to an acquaintance of an acquaintance, a woman I'd never met. In an email she told me that the room was very small, with a kitchenette and bathroom, warning me too about the traffic and the neon ads. What she didn't mention was that the building was a refuge, run by a charity that rented out cheap single rooms to working professionals in addition to housing a more or less permanent population of the long-term homeless, particularly those with Aids and serious mental health problems. This was explained to me by one of the two security guards on the front desk, who gave me the white electronic card I needed to enter and exit the lobby and who took me up to the room to show me how to operate the locks. He'd just started the job, and in the elevator he told me about the building's population, saying of things I might or might not see *if we're not worried about it you don't need to be.*

The halls were painted a hospital green and lit red and white by wall lights, ceiling lights and EXIT signs. My room was just big enough to fit a futon and a desk, a microwave, a sink and a small fridge. There were Mardi Gras beads hanging in the bathroom, and the walls were lined with books and toys. Reggae gave way to a baseball game through the thin wall, and outside crowds of people surged intermittently up from the subway at Port Authority.

I'd taken the room because it was cheap and because of a photograph I'd grown obsessed with that spring. It was shot a single block away in the summer of 1979 and shows a man standing outside the 7th Avenue exit of the Times Square–42nd Street subway. He's wearing a sleeveless denim jacket, a white T-shirt and a paper mask of Arthur Rimbaud, a life-sized photocopy of the famous portrait on the cover of *Illuminations*. Behind him a man with an Afro is jaywalking in a billowing white shirt and flared black pants. The shutter has caught him mid-bounce, one shoe still in the air. Both sides of the street are lined with big old-timey cars and cinemas. *Moonraker* is on at the New Amsterdam, *Amityville Horror* at the Harris, while the sign at the Victory, just above Rimbaud's head, promises in big black letters RATED X.

It's The Deuce, of course: the old name for that stretch of 42nd Street which runs between 6th and 8th Avenue, and which was at the time one of the vice capitals of the world. In the 1970s the city of New York was almost bankrupt and beset by violence and crime. Times Square was populated by prostitutes, dealers, pimps and hustlers, and the old Beaux-Arts theatres had been turned into porn cinemas and cruising grounds.

What better place for Rimbaud? He looks entirely at home there, his paper face expressionless, the gutter glinting at his feet. In other images from the series, which is entitled *Arthur Rimbaud in New York*, he shoots heroin, rides the subway, masturbates in bed, eats in a diner, poses with carcasses at a slaughterhouse, and wanders through the wreckage of the Hudson piers, lounging with outstretched arms in front of a wall spray-painted with the words THE SILENCE OF MARCEL DUCHAMP IS OVERRATED.

The photographs are black and white, beautifully composed silver gelatin prints. Though their setting is recognizably New York, they seem to report from some decaying dream city, a mythic place of violence and danger. In the 42nd Street shot a single silhouetted hand protrudes from Rimbaud's side. Someone's crossing behind him, at once captured and effaced. At the end of the road the sky glows mercury white, enshrouding the furthest buildings in a misty, apocalyptic light.

The character of Rimbaud was played by various men, but the series was conceived, orchestrated and shot in its entirety by David Wojnarowicz, a then-unknown New Yorker who would in a few years become one of the stars of the East Village art scene, alongside contemporaries like Jean-Michel Basquiat, Keith Haring and Kiki Smith. I'd encountered Wojnarowicz by way of my friend, the film-maker Matt Wolf, and had spent the past few months immersed in the extraordinary body of work – paintings, installations, films, photographs and books – he produced before dying of Aids in 1992, at the age of thirty-seven.

Rimbaud was his first serious project. In an interview years later he talked about its origins, saying, 'I've periodically found myself in situations that felt desperate and, in those moments, I'd feel that I needed to make certain things . . . I had Rimbaud come through a vague biographical outline of what my past had been – the places I had hung out in as a kid, the places I starved in or haunted on some level.'

He wasn't kidding about the desperate situations. His parents divorced when he was two, and for a time he and his two siblings were left in a boarding house, where they were physically abused. Their mother had custody, but when David was four or so the children were kidnapped by their father, an alcoholic sailor who worked on passenger ships. Ed took them to live with his new wife in the suburbs of New Jersey, in what David later described as the Universe of the Neatly Clipped Lawn – a place where physical and psychic violence against women, queers and children could be carried out without repercussions.

'In my home,' he wrote in his memoir, *Close to the Knives,* 'one could not laugh, one could not express boredom, one could not cry, one could not play, one could not explore, one could not engage in any activity that showed development or growth that was independent.' Ed was away for weeks at a time, but when he was at home he terrorized the children. David remembered being beaten with dog leashes and two-by-fours; remembered his sister being slammed on the sidewalk until brown liquid oozed from her ears, while neighbours pruned their gardens and mowed their lawns.

In the mid-1960s all three kids either ran away to or were dumped on their mother, who was living in Manhattan, in a tiny apartment in Hell's Kitchen. Dolores was emotionally warmer than her former husband, but she was also erratic and struggled with the burden of raising her by now troubled children. At fifteen, David was turning ten-dollar tricks in Times Square, and by seventeen had left home entirely. He almost starved while living on the street. Later he'd remember his gums bleeding each time he smoked a cigarette. He never got enough sleep, either. Sometimes he'd spend the night on the roof of buildings, curled against the heating vents, and in the morning would wake covered in soot, his eyes and mouth and nose filled with a choking black dust.

What did it mean, to go back to those places and insert Rimbaud into the landscape of his childhood, to have him stand impassively by the painted barrier where David used to lean as a boy, waiting for ageing men to buy his skinny, unkempt body? That double-edged word *haunted* kept tugging at me. I'd been thinking a lot that winter about why people make art, and what it means when it outlives them.

About cities, too: their empty spaces, the things they hide. Who knows how time works? David died over twenty years ago, but some nights, lying in the oily glow of the Jumbotron, it seemed not only possible but certain that the Rimbaud he'd created was still at large in the streets beneath me, passing anonymously between the men who wandered like moths in and out of the peep-show lights.

I'd come to New York to visit the Wojnarowicz archive at Fales Library, which is housed inside the big Bobst Library at New York University. Each morning I walked forty blocks down Broadway and 5th to Washington Square, picking up a coffee on the way. It was unseasonably cold that spring, just as it had been unseasonably hot the year before. At the library I'd show my pass and take the elevator to the third floor, deposit my illegal pens in a locker and borrow a pencil to fill out a request sheet. Series I, Journals. Series VIII, Audio. Series IX, Photographs. Series XIII, Objects.

Over the course of three weeks, I photographed thirty-eight journals, occasionally dislodging old menus and receipts. I watched six films, most of them unfinished. I wrote down dreams, and in the evenings, when I walked home, my mind would be filled with images that had surfaced long ago, in the looking glass of someone else's mind. A beluga whale, drifting through grains and sheaves of light. A man shooting heroin on an abandoned pier, tumbling out of consciousness, limp and lovely as a Pietà, spit bubbling from his lips. Dreams of an underground lake, receding down a country road. Dreams of fucking. Dreams of horses. Dreams of dying tarantulas. Dreams of snakes.

For two full days I unpacked boxes of objects, each item loosely wrapped in crumples of white paper. There were boxes of figurines, boxes of Halloween masks and model cars, model guns, toy dinosaurs and armadillos. Some I recognized from films; some were so repulsive – a plaster cast of a tongue licking an ear, life-sized and painted a faecal green – that it was hard to bring myself to touch them. Others were so charismatic it took all my willpower not to slip them into my pocket. I kept taking photographs of a little wooden mask, its crude face calm, its surface stippled with leopard spots. The boxes formed a kind of artwork in their own right: a time capsule arranged around the missing presence of the artist.

Much of David's work after his diagnosis is about disappearances of one kind or another. Maybe that's a stupid thing to say, given the breadth and complexity of his art. But even a casual glance reveals things slipping out of sight, heading toward extinction. The ants in *A Fire in My Belly*, say, or the tiny frog in *What Is This Little Guy's Job in the World*, sitting patiently in a giant human hand. His most famous photograph, which appears on the cover of U2's *One*, shows a diorama of buffalo hurtling off a cliff. And the last thing he ever made was an image of his own face almost completely buried in dirt, his eyes screwed shut, his big teeth bared, like someone waiting for a blow to come.

He was diagnosed with ARC (a soon-to-be outmoded term meaning Aids-related complex) in the spring of 1988, a few months after his best friend – soulmate, former lover, teacher, surrogate father, surrogate brother – died of the disease, after a long and vicious illness. Peter Hujar was a famously brilliant, famously difficult photographer, and his protection and love helped David step aside at least a little from the burdens of his childhood.

He filmed the beluga whales in their tank at the Bronx Zoo a few days after Peter died, mixing them with Super 8 footage of his dead body lying in a spotted gown on a hospital bed. I'd watched it on one of the monitors at Fales. The camera sweeps up and down, settling on Peter's beautiful hand, a hospital bracelet looped around his emaciated wrist. Later, there's a re-enactment of a dream: a shirtless man being passed through a chain of shirtless men, his supine body slipping gently from hand to tender hand.

Peter's was one death in a matrix of thousands of deaths, one loss among thousands of losses. It makes no sense to consider it in isolation. Between 1981 and 1996, when combination therapy became available, over 80,000 people died of Aids in New York City, most of them gay men, in conditions of the most horrifying ignorance and fear. Patients were left to die on gurneys in hospital corridors. Nurses refused to treat them, funeral parlours to bury their bodies. Politicians blocked funding and education, while public figures called for those with Aids to be tattooed with their infection status or quarantined on islands. Hardly any wonder David described being filled with rage like a blood-filled egg, or fantasized about growing to superhuman size and wreaking vengeance on those who considered his life and the lives of those he loved expendable.

In the archive, I watched *Silence = Death*, a documentary made by Rosa von Praunheim in the early years of the epidemic. David appeared repeatedly: a tall, rangy man in glasses, wearing a white T-shirt hand-painted with the words FUCK ME SAFE. He spoke in his deep, agitated voice about what it feels like to live with homophobia and hypocritical politicians, to watch your friends die and to know that your own body contains a virus that will kill you. Sometimes his words were overlaid against footage containing items now stored in the boxes I was working on. A rotatable globe, packed in tissue, Box 19.

What struck me, watching him speak – what, I suppose, had drawn me all the way across the Atlantic – was the intensity of his anger, the way he spoke up in all his work for those who were, because of their sexuality, because of the particularity of their desires, rendered voiceless and invisible. In an era in which people with Aids tended to be portrayed as helpless and isolated, dying wasted and alone, he refused the identity of victim. Instead, he set about explaining, in rapid, lucid sentences, how the virus revealed another kind of sickness, at work inside the system of America itself.

Like many East Village artists, among them Keith Haring, Zoe Leonard and Gregg Bordowitz, he was a member of ACT UP: a direct action group established in New York in 1987. ACT UP, which stands for Aids Coalition to Unleash Power, tackled multiple aspects of the crisis. Among their many actions, they protested the Catholic Church's stand against safe-sex education in New York public schools and used sit-ins to force pharmaceutical companies to make medication affordable and to open clinical trials to drug addicts and women.

Before I left England, I'd gone to a screening of *United in Anger*, a documentary about ACT UP's remarkable work by two of its surviving members, the writer Sarah Schulman and the film-maker Jim Hubbard. It was stitched together from contemporary footage, and every once in a while, I'd see David standing at the back of a protest, identifiable by his height and by the jacket that he wore, on the back of which was printed a pink triangle and the words IF I DIE OF AIDS – FORGET BURIAL – JUST DROP MY BODY ON THE STEPS OF THE F.D.A. – a reference to the Food and Drug Administration's failure to confront the epidemic.

One of the slogans chanted at those protests was *I'll never be silent again*. Hearing it, I was flooded with memories of my first Gay Pride parade, sometime in the late 1980s. I'd been taken by my lesbian mother, with a hand-painted banner on a pillowcase. I must have been eleven, I guess. *I'll never be silent again*. We'd just moved to Portsmouth from Buckinghamshire, after she'd been outed among the parents at the Catholic convent school I'd gone to all my life. I'd grown up in the closet, and though I didn't know anything then about Aids, I knew how liberating it felt to be chanting about silence on Waterloo Bridge, part of a thousand-strong army of dykes and queens.

I'll tell you what I did know. I knew what homophobia meant. I knew what even one person's disgust at someone else's sexuality could cost in terms of homes and jobs, security and peace of mind. But I was raised in the country, and almost exclusively by women. Aids was not an immediate part of our world. It sank in slowly. I remember a boy wearing a badge saying LOVE AND PASSION IS STILL IN FASHION. I remember my grief when Freddie Mercury died. And then, as a teenager, it came into sharper focus. I remember reading *Fucking Martin*, and Derek Jarman's diaries, sobbing with anger at the pointless grotesquery of his death. But I was lucky. I didn't lose friends or loved ones. I've had several Aids tests in the last two decades, but I became sexually active after combination therapy, when, in the West at least, the worst of the plague years had ended.

As I worked my way through the archive, I kept thinking about what it means to be the generation that comes after, growing up with the knowledge that there are legions of missing persons, that one's tribe is full of ghosts. What are our responsibilities? Are we witnesses or voyeurs to someone else's incalculable losses? I don't have answers to these questions, but I turn them over all the time.

Towards the end of my stay in the library, I ordered up David's audio journals. Over the past few years I'd grown accustomed to picking through the most intimate papers of the dead, but nothing prepared me for the intensity of listening to those tapes. Many were recorded on waking, or in the middle stretches of the night. Often you could hear car horns and sirens, people talking on the street outside. Then David's deep voice, struggling upward out of sleep. He talks about his work and his sexuality and sometimes he walks to the window, opens the curtains and reports on what he sees there. A man in the apartment opposite, combing his hair beneath a bare bulb. A dark-haired stranger standing outside the Chinese laundry, who meets his eyes and doesn't break the gaze. He talks about what dying will feel like, about whether it will be frightening or painful. He says he hopes it will be like slipping into warm water, and then on the crackling tape he starts to sing: low plaintive notes, rising and falling over the surf of morning traffic.

One night, he wakes after a bad dream and switches on the machine to talk it out. He's dreamt about a horse being caught in some train tracks, its spine broken, unable to escape. 'It was very much alive,' he says, 'and it was just so fucking upsetting to see this thing.' He describes how he tried to free it, and how instead it was dragged into a wall and skinned alive. 'I haven't the faintest idea what it means for me. And I feel horror and a very deep sadness about something. Whatever the tone of the dream carries it was just so sad and so shocking.' He says goodbye then, and shuts the machine off.

Something alive, something alive and lovely caught and damaged in the mechanisms, the gears and rails of society. When I think about Aids, when I think about the people who have died, and the conditions they experienced, when I think about those who have survived and who carry inside themselves a decade of mourning, a decade of missing people, I think of David's dream. When I cried while listening to the tapes, which I did periodically, surreptitiously wiping my eyes on my sleeve, it wasn't just out of sadness, or pity. It was out of rage, that I lived in a world in which this kind of mass death had been permitted, in which nobody in a position of power had stopped the train and freed the horse in time.

If I say to you these names, if I say Peter Hujar, Arthur Russell, Klaus Nomi, Cookie Mueller, Derek Jarman, Jack Smith, Keith Haring, Robert Mapplethorpe, do you know who I mean? Multiply them by ten thousand. Now answer me this: how do we begin to calculate what we have lost?

It got colder and colder. One night, walking home at 2.30 in the morning, I saw a carriage horse bolting down a deserted 43rd Street. Another evening, I passed in the crowd on 42nd a man shouting to no one in particular *New York! We're drowning in colours!* I grew accustomed to the repeating patterns of the neighbourhood: the camera stores, the shops that sold tchotchkes for tourists, the corner delis with their plastic tubs of tasteless tropical fruit. In the elevator at the Times Square Hotel, I stepped in and out of conversations. Two women interrogating a man with greased-back hair about Louis Vuitton bags. *What colour you want? Black. When you going? She's going in an hour and a half.*

Every city is a place of disappearances, but Manhattan is an island, and to reinvent itself must literally bulldoze the past. The Times Square of the Rimbaud photo, the Times Square of David's youth, had in the intervening decades undergone a drastic shift. The porn cinemas were long gone, replaced by corporate offices and high-end magazines. The Victory, which in the Rimbaud photo was screening

X-rated movies, was now a gleamingly restored children's theatre, while the New Amsterdam was owned by Disney and had shown nothing but *Mary Poppins* since 2006.

During the long, lit evenings, I pored over books about New York's gentrification, and how it intersects with Aids. Sarah Schulman's extraordinary polemic, *Gentrification of the Mind*, had just been published. In it, she explains how the thousands of Aids deaths freed up rent-controlled apartments in Manhattan to market rates, since at the time homosexual partners could not inherit leases, even of homes they'd inhabited for years. David did manage to cling on to Peter Hujar's place, but only after a gruelling legal battle. And even then, he spent the last three years of his life being tormented by the developers transforming the Yiddish theatre downstairs into a multiplex. They damaged his possessions, flooded the apartment and filled the building with dust and noise.

It's ironic that Manhattan is becoming a kind of gated island for the super-rich, when one considers that in the 1970s it was closer to a gated prison for the poor, its reputation as a danger zone exploited in the 1981 sci-fi film *Escape from New York*. The more I heard about its changes, the more I realized that the building I was staying in represented an anomaly, an anachronistic holdout against the march of the developers. The Times Square Hotel was at the time in the third of its incarnations, and its history encapsulated the neighbourhood's uneasy accommodations between capital and enterprise, poverty and need.

Built like an art deco liner, with fifteen storeys and a marble ballroom, it opened in 1924, slipping over the decades from glamour to a faded gentility. By the 1970s it housed a long-term population of mostly elderly residents. In this period, homelessness had reached crisis point in New York City, and housing agencies began to employ hotels as temporary lodgings for the destitute and vulnerable. The Times Square became a welfare hotel, its empty rooms used to warehouse the overflow from the city's teeming shelters. In *7 Miles a Second*, a graphic novel about his childhood, David remembered times when he was forced to stay in such places, with rotting mattresses and doors sawed two foot from the floor, so any creep could crawl in while you slept. Even exhausted, he preferred the relative openness of the streets.

I don't know if he ever visited the Times Square itself, but as a kid he certainly turned tricks in places like it. He wrote about them later: the middle-aged men who'd pick him up, the grubby little rooms they'd take him to. One time, the john made him watch another couple through a peephole in the wall. When the woman turned around he saw there were unhealed knife wounds all over her belly. In *7 Miles a Second*, there's a picture of her torso, coloured in inked swatches of red and pink and brown. 'What really twisted my brain,' kid David says, 'was how that guy could fuck that woman' – a hooker he recognized from outside Port Authority – 'with those fresh wounds staring him in the face! Like he couldn't conceive of pain attached to the body he was fucking.'

This is what the Times Square Alliance is supposed to have erased: the panhandlers, the hookers and hustlers, the damaged and hungry bodies. And yet, by some quirk, the hotel itself had run counter to the tide. By the 1990s it was virtually a no-go zone, teetering on bankruptcy and in violation of hundreds of housing, health and fire codes. For most buildings in the area, this spelled the beginning of gentrification: the relentless cycles of eviction, demolition and refurbishment. But the Times Square Hotel caught the eye of Rosanne Haggerty, a recent college graduate who became obsessed with restoring the building. Haggerty established the charity Common Ground and succeeded in turning the hotel into what is now the largest permanent supportive housing residence in America: a refuge for the vulnerable population it had once housed so precariously.

Every day I encountered people in wheelchairs and on crutches, people missing limbs, people with burns like brands running up their arms. It was recognizably the same world that David had inhabited. Though in time he lost some of his attraction to the chaos of street life, he remained attentive to its citizens, alert to the hurt and the dispossessed. His first book, *Sounds in the Distance*, is a collection of monologues recorded from people he encountered at one or two or three in the morning, out on the piers, or in dive bars, bus stations and coffee shops. In 'Twenty-Year-Old Woman in Times Square' a hooker talks about having her arms slashed by a trick with a knife. *Look at this*, she says. *I fuckin wrapped them up but they haven't stopped bleeding.* He doesn't objectify his people, but instead lets them speak for themselves, amplifying their voices into print. It's not voyeuristic, I don't think, but rather a raw, defiant way of bearing witness, to a larger and more perilous America than we like to think exists.

Times Square itself might have been sanitized, but the old street life was still going on around the margins. The archive was closed at weekends, and so I went for long walks around the neighbourhood, drifting through Midtown and Hell's Kitchen and on to the wreckage of the Hudson piers. Most of those walks have melted into one another, but one remains distinct. It was St Patrick's Day. In the morning Times Square was filled with drunken teenagers in green baseball caps, and I walked right down to Tompkins Square Park to escape them. By the time I turned for home it had begun to snow and the streets were almost deserted.

At Broadway and 39th I passed a man sitting in a doorway, crying. He must have been in his forties, with cropped hair and big cracked hands. I went over to ask if he was OK. He said that he'd been sitting there three days and not a single person had stopped to speak to him. He told me about his kids – *I got three beautiful babies on Long Island* – and then a confusing story about work boots. He showed me a wound on his arm and said *I got stabbed yesterday. I'm like a piece of shit here. People throw pennies at me.* It was snowing hard, the flakes whirling down. My hair was soaked already. After a while, I gave him five bucks and walked on. That night I watched the snow falling for a long time. The air was full of wet neon, sliding and smearing in the streets. What is it about the pain of others? It's not like it's infectious, is it?

I'd come to the Wojnarowicz archive to see the Magic Box, but for two weeks I kept putting it off. It wasn't until the Monday after St Patrick's Day that I finally called it up. According to his boyfriend, Tom Rauffenbart, David kept the box under his bed at Hujar's loft, never discussing its function or significance. It had its own subcategory in the finding aid. Series XIII, Subseries B, The Magic Box.

It was made of pine, the wood stained here and there with water. The sides read FLORIDA'S FINEST CITRUS in looping red cursive and the top said INDIAN RIVER CITRUS above a jolly frieze of cut oranges and sunbeams and distant orange groves. Someone had stuck a strip of masking tape above the trees, and written on it in crayon MAGIC BOX.

I pulled on my itchy cotton gloves and slid the lid open. Inside, there was a jumble of objects, the sort of miscellaneous hoard you might find at a car boot sale or flea market stall. I lifted them out one by one, making messy, vaguely colour-coded piles across the table. A tin crocodile with a feather in his mouth. A river stone. A red plastic cowboy. A rose quartz, an unopened bag of toy bugs, a cotton snake, a crucifix. Dime beads, a Joker, an envelope of pesos. Fistfuls of necklaces, a glittery snowman in a top hat. Rings, penknives, a knuckle of malachite, a watch, some toothpicks, a plastic box of dried flowers and little shells and bones. Three model steam trains. Two grinning skulls with diamanté eyes. A watermelon key ring, its chain a little rusted. The curator came over then, and asked if I'd smelled inside. I stuck my nose in. Musk and incense, cut with the lingering scent of oranges and cigarettes.

No one knows exactly what the Magic Box was for. An amulet, maybe. Some kind of protective spell against all the bad things that kept crowding in. Perhaps it was meant to exert a benign, calming influence, on the nights when David woke, heart pounding, convinced a serial killer was prowling through his room. It wasn't just the disease that had him by the throat. Three years before he died, he got caught up in one of the most gruelling and public battles of the culture war. Some of his collages, which contained miniature photos of sexual activity, were used by the right-wing American Family Association as a way of discrediting the National Endowment for the Arts. In the end, David took the AFA to court for taking his images out of context, winning a landmark case about how an artist's work can be reproduced and used.

I'd read his testimony from the trial. He talked with an intense eloquence about his paintings, explaining the context and meaning of all their intricate parts. In addition, he addressed the use of explicit imagery in his work, telling the judge, 'I use images of sexuality to deal with what I have experienced, and the fact that I think sexuality and the human body should not be a taboo subject this late in the twentieth century. I also use images of sexuality to portray the diversity of people, and their sexual orientations, and one of the biggest reasons I feel uncomfortable about the idea of the human body being a taboo subject is that, had the human body not been a taboo subject in this decade, I might have gotten the information from the Health Department, from elected representatives, that would have spared me having contracted this virus.'

The human body: that imperfect, desiring, desirable, wounded object. In his memoir *Close to the Knives*, he elaborated on this train of thought, writing:

> I discovered making things meant leaving evidence of life behind when I moved on. Making things was like leaving historical records of my existence behind when I left the room, or building, or neighborhood, the state and possibly the earth . . . as in mortality, as in death. When I was a kid I discovered that making an object, whether it was a drawing or a story, meant making something that spoke even if I was silent. As an adult, I realize if I make something and leave it in public for any period of time, I can create an environment where that object or writing acts as a magnet and draws others with a similar frame of reference out of silence or invisibility . . . To place an object or writing that contains what is invisible because of legislation or social taboo into an environment outside myself makes me feel not so alone; it keeps me company

by virtue of its existence. It is kind of like a ventriloquist's dummy
– the only difference is that the work can speak by itself or act like
that 'magnet' to attract others who carried this enforced silence.

There are many things I could say about the Magic Box. I could say
that it seemed to me, like much of David's work, to form a kind of
occult counter-history of America, packed with the ritual objects of
its rival tribes. I could say that when I opened it, I remembered the
persistent myth that Manhattan Island was bought from the Canarsie
Indians for a box of beads and other trinkets, and that I sometimes
wondered about the kind of city the Magic Box might purchase.
I could say that when I'd unpacked all the objects, I looked at them
and felt, for the hundredth time that month, sick with rage that this
courageous, sexy, radical, difficult, immensely talented man died at
the age of thirty-seven. But none of these statements would tell you
how it felt to see the things that David had assembled, in the face of
his own oncoming death. They settled in my heart, as I expect they
have settled in the heart of everyone who's seen them.

Here: you can have them too. Take them as a spell against silence,
a prophylactic to repel prejudice. Tin crocodile, river stone, red plastic
cowboy: a talisman to ward off fear, to cast out shame. It's still here,
I guess is what I'm saying. Against the odds, you can still touch it. ∎

PARADISE LOST

Nathan Thornburgh

Maybe at first I didn't appreciate the taxi driver, because of the way he careened down the coastline. Although, really, what a way it would have been to die. Such beauty. He would have reached over to light his cigarette, or change the tape in the tape deck, his hand would slip on the wheel, and the green forests of Abkhazia would rush at me at seventy miles an hour as the Lada jumped the guard rail. The car would take flight and in the distance I would see the jagged snow-covered peaks, home of mountain monasteries, spiral upside down as the Lada began to flip. The car would level for a weightless instant, and then plunge over the slate cliff and toward the lapis lazuli waters of the Black Sea below.

All of Abkhazia's natural gifts – mountain, forest, coastline – would make a gorgeous backdrop for the death that I and the driver had coming anyway.

But I didn't die, and truth be told, I didn't even get very close in his taxi, so maybe it was something else that bugged me. Was it the music he played? It came through that tinny tape deck and was incessant and mournful and patriotic about the war the Abkhaz call the Patriotic War – *Those who were with us were with us, and those who were against us were against us.*

Music became a sore subject for us after a week in Abkhazia. In an otherwise empty restaurant, the music was as loud as an air-raid siren and the owner looked at me stiffly when we asked if it could be turned down just a little bit. Then the owner said no, and it was suddenly clear that this is what war did. He had probably fought and lost loved ones and won and the Abkhaz were now free, and even though the war ended twenty years ago he still remembered every nauseous moment and the lesson for him was that the Abkhaz won the war and that meant that he could play his shitty ballads in his empty restaurant and crank it so loud that his only customers had to leave, and that was OK, because Abkhazia was free.

The photographer Yuri Kozyrev is with me on this trip to Abkhazia in late 2011, travelling south along that fabled coastline, up into the mountains and down to the tense Georgian border in Gali. Kozyrev had been in Abkhazia during the war; it's my first visit. We're both, however, struck by how time just seems to stand still there. A rusting trawler, an empty restaurant, a half-deserted coast. Even the national pastime is sleepy: the Abkhaz are famous for their skill at dominoes.

And yet, under the sleepiness is violence. 'Abkhaz democracy reminds me a lot of America,' an Abkhaz journalist tells me over coffee. 'It's a democracy of heavily armed people.' ∎

PARADISE LOST

Yuri Kozyrev

1. Abkhaz troops in Sukhumi, Abkhazia's capital.

2. Ramas Beraia, an ethnic Georgian, lost his leg after stepping on a landmine on the banks of the Inguri River.

3. The former parliament building in Sukhumi.

4. Abkhaz soldiers train at the Military Academy in Sukhumi.

5. Ethnic Georgian children perform a traditional dance at the Didtsifuri school in the village of Dikhazurga.

6. Abkhaz boys play in a hot spring in Ochamchire.

7. Nowadays, the once-thriving tourism industry consists of Russian soldiers and retirees on cheap holidays.

8. An Abkhaz man at an abandoned house where a Georgian family used to live.

9. A boy jumps from an abandoned Turkish freighter beached near central Sukhumi.

10. Abkhaz children in Ochamchire, which used to be populated predominantly by ethnic Georgians.

11. Russian tourists are regular visitors to the sanatoriums along the Gagra seashore.

enjoying yourself?

GRANTA

THE MAGAZINE OF NEW WRITING

SUBSCRIPTION FORM FOR UK, EUROPE AND REST OF THE WORLD

Yes, I would like to take out a subscription to *Granta*.

GUARANTEE: If I am ever dissatisfied with my *Granta* subscription, I will simply notify you, and you will send me a complete refund or credit my credit card, as applicable, for all un-mailed issues.

YOUR DETAILS

MR / MISS / MRS / DR ....
NAME ....
ADDRESS ....
....
POSTCODE ....
EMAIL ....

☐ Please tick this box if you do not wish to receive special offers from *Granta*
☐ Please tick this box if you do not wish to receive offers from organizations selected by *Granta*

YOUR PAYMENT DETAILS

1) ☐ Pay £32 (saving £20) by Direct Debit
   To pay by Direct Debit please complete the mandate and return to the address shown below.

2) Pay by cheque or credit/debit card. Please complete below:

   1 year subscription: ☐ UK: £36   ☐ Europe: £42   ☐ Rest of World: £46

   3 year subscription: ☐ UK: £99   ☐ Europe: £108   ☐ Rest of World: £126

   I wish to pay by   ☐ CHEQUE   ☐ CREDIT/DEBIT CARD
   Cheque enclosed for £_____ made payable to *Granta*.

   Please charge £ _____ to my: ☐ Visa   ☐ MasterCard   ☐ Amex   ☐ Switch/Maestro

   Card No. ☐☐☐☐☐☐☐☐☐☐☐☐☐☐☐☐☐☐☐

   Valid from *(if applicable)* ☐☐☐☐   Expiry Date ☐☐☐☐   Issue No. ☐☐

   Security No. ☐☐☐

SIGNATURE .... DATE ....

Instructions to your Bank or Building Society to pay by Direct Debit
BANK NAME ....
BANK ADDRESS ....
POSTCODE ....
ACCOUNT IN THE NAMES(S) OF: ....
SIGNED ....
DATE ....

DIRECT Debit

Instructions to your Bank or Building Society: Please pay Granta Publications direct debits from the account detailed on this instruction subject to the safeguards assured by the direct debit guarantee. I understand that this instruction may remain with Granta and, if so, details will be passed electronically to my bank/building society. Banks and building societies may not accept direct debit instructions from some types of account.

Bank/building society account number
☐☐☐☐☐☐☐☐

Sort Code
☐☐☐☐☐☐

Originator's Identification
☐9☐1☐3☐1☐3☐3

Please mail this order form with payment instructions to:

Granta Publications
12 Addison Avenue
London, W11 4QR
Or call +44(0)208 955 7011
or visit GRANTA.COM

THANK YOU FOR HAVING ME

Lorrie Moore

The day following Michael Jackson's death, I was constructing my own memorial for him. I played his videos on YouTube and sat in the kitchen at night, with the iPod light at the table's centre the only source of illumination. I listened to 'Man in the Mirror' and 'Ben', my favourite, even if it was about a killer rat. I tried not to think about its being about a rat, as it was also the name of an old beau, who had emailed me from Istanbul upon hearing of Jackson's death. Apparently there was no one in Turkey to talk about it with. 'When I heard the news of MJackson's death I thought of you,' the ex-beau had written, 'and that sweet, loose-limbed dance you used to do to one of his up-tempo numbers.'

I tried to think positively. 'Well, at least Whitney Houston didn't die,' I said to someone on the phone. Every minute that ticked by in life contained very little information, until suddenly it contained too much.

'Mom, what are you doing?' asked my fifteen-year-old daughter, Nickie. 'You look like a crazy lady sitting in the kitchen like this.'

'I'm just listening to some music.'

'But like this?'

'I didn't want to disturb you.'

'You are so totally disturbing me,' she said.

Nickie had lately announced a desire to have her own reality show so that the world could see what she had to put up with.

I pulled out the earbuds. 'What are you wearing tomorrow?'

'Whatever. I mean, does it matter?'

'Uh, no. Not really.' Nickie sauntered out of the room. Of course it did not matter what young people wore: they were already amazing looking, without really knowing it, which was also part of their beauty. I was going to be Nickie's date at the wedding of Maria, her former babysitter, and Nickie was going to be mine. The person who needed to be careful what she wore was me.

It was a wedding in the country, a half-hour drive, and we arrived on time, but somehow we seemed the last ones there. Guests milled about semi-purposefully. Maria, an attractive, restless Brazilian, was marrying a local farm boy, for the second time – a second farm boy on a second farm. The previous farm boy she had married, Ian, was present as well. He had been hired to play music, and as the guests floated by with their plastic cups of wine, Ian sat there playing a slow melancholic version of 'I Want You Back'. Except he didn't seem to want her back. He was smiling and nodding at everyone and seemed happy to be part of this send-off. He was the entertainment. He wore a T-shirt that read, THANK YOU FOR HAVING ME. This seemed remarkably sanguine and useful as well as a little beautiful. I wondered how it was done. I myself had never done anything remotely similar. 'Marriage is one long conversation,' wrote Robert Louis Stevenson. Of course, he was dead at forty-four, so he had no idea how long it could really get to be.

'I can't believe you wore that,' Nickie whispered to me in her mauve eyelet sundress.

'I know. It probably was a mistake.' I was wearing a synthetic leopard-print sheath: I admired camouflage. A leopard's markings I'd imagined existed because a leopard's habitat had once been alive with snakes, and blending in was required. Leopards were frightened of snakes and also of chimpanzees, who were in turn frightened of leopards – a stand-off between predator and prey, since there was a confusion as to which was which: this was also a theme in the wilds of my closet. Perhaps I had watched too many nature documentaries.

'Maybe you could get Ian some lemonade,' I said to Nickie. I had already grabbed some wine from a passing black plastic tray.

'Yes, maybe I could,' she said and loped across the yard. I watched her broad tan back and her confident gait. She was a gorgeous giantess. I was in awe to have such a daughter. Also in fear – as in fearful for my life.

'It's good you and Maria have stayed friends,' I said to Ian. Ian's father, who had one of those embarrassing father-in-law crushes on his son's departing wife, was not taking it so well. One could see him misty-eyed, treading the edge of the property with some iced gin, keeping his eye out for Maria, waiting for her to come out of the house, waiting for an opening, when she might be free of others, so he could rush up and embrace her.

'Yes.' Ian smiled. Ian sighed. And for a fleeting moment everything felt completely fucked up.

And then everything righted itself again. It felt important spiritually to go to weddings: to give balance to the wakes and memorial services. People shouldn't have been set in motion on this planet only to grieve losses. And without weddings there were only funerals. I had seen a soccer mom become a rhododendron with a plaque, next to the soccer field parking lot, as if it had been watching all those matches that had killed her. I had seen a brilliant young student become a creative writing contest, as if it were all that writing that had been the thing to do him in. And I had seen a public defender become a justice fund, as if one paid for fairness with one's very life. I had seen a dozen people become hunks of rock with their names engraved so shockingly perfectly upon the surface it looked as if they had indeed turned to stone, been given a new life the way the moon is given it, through some lighting tricks and a face-like font. I had turned a hundred Rolodex cards around to their blank sides. So let a babysitter become a bride again. Let her marry over and over. So much urgent and lifelike love went rumbling around underground and died there, never got expressed at all, so let some errant inconvenient attraction have its way. There was so little time.

Someone very swanky and tall and in muddy high heels in the grass was now standing in front of Ian, holding a microphone, and singing 'Waters of March' while Ian accompanied. My mind imitated the song by wandering: A stick. A stone. A wad of cow pie. A teary mom's eye.

'There are a bazillion Brazilians here,' said Nickie, arriving with two lemonades.

'What did you expect?' I took one of the lemonades for Ian and put my arm around her.

'I don't know. I only ever met her sister. Just once. The upside is at least I'm not the only one wearing a colour.'

We gazed across the long yard of the farmhouse. Maria's sister and her mother were by the rose bushes, having their pictures taken without the bride.

'Maria and her sister both look like their mother.' Her mother and I had met once before, and I now nodded in her direction across the yard. I couldn't tell if she could see me.

Nickie nodded with a slight smirk. 'Their father died in a car crash. So yeah, they don't look like him.'

I swatted her arm. 'Nickie. Sheesh.'

She was silent for a while. 'Do you ever think of Dad?'

'Dad who?'

'Come on.'

'You mean, Dad-eeeeee?'

The weekend her father left – left the house, the town, the country, everything, packing so lightly I believed he would come back – he had said, 'You can raise Nickie by yourself. You'll be good at it.'

And I had said, 'Are you on crack?'

And he had replied, continuing to fold a blue twill jacket, 'Yes, a little.'

'Dadder. As in *badder*,' Nickie said now. She sometimes claimed to friends that her father had died, and when she was asked how, she would gaze bereavedly off into the distance and say, 'A really, really serious game of Hangman.' Mothers and their only children of divorce were a skewed family dynamic, if they were families at all. Perhaps they were more like cruddy buddy movies, and the dialogue between them was unrecognizable as filial or parental. It was extraterrestrial. With a streak of dog-walkers-meeting-at-the-park. It contained more sibling banter than it should have. Still, I preferred the whole thing to being a lonely old spinster, the fate I once thought I was most genetically destined for, though I'd worked hard, too hard, to defy and avoid it, when perhaps there it lay ahead of me regardless. If you were alone when you were born, alone when you were dying, *really absolutely* alone when you were dead, why 'learn to be alone' in between? If you had forgotten, it would quickly come back to you. Aloneness was like riding a bike. At gunpoint. With the gun in your own hand. Aloneness was the air in your tyres, the wind in your hair. You didn't have to go looking for it with open arms. With open arms, you fell off the bike: I was drinking my wine too quickly.

Maria came out of the house in her beautiful shoulderless wedding dress, which was white as could be.

'What a fantastic costume,' said Nickie archly.

Nickie was both keen observer and enthusiastic participant in the sartorial disguise department, and when she was little there had been much playing of Wedding, fake bridal bouquets made of ragged plastic-handled sponges tossed up into the air and often into the garage basketball hoop, catching there. She was also into Halloween. She would trick-or-treat for UNICEF dressed in a sniper outfit or a suicide bomber outfit replete with vest. Once when she was eight, she went as a dryad, a tree nymph, and when asked at doors what she was, she kept saying, 'A tree-nip.' She had been a haughty trick-or-treater, alert to the failed adult guessing game of it – *you're a what? a vampire?* – so when the neighbours looked confused, she scowled and said reproachfully, 'Have you *never* studied Greek mythology?' Nickie knew how to terrify. She had sometimes been more interested in answering our own door than in knocking on others, peering around the edge of it with a witch hat and a loud cackle. 'I think it's time to get back to the customers,' she announced to me one Halloween when she was five, grabbing my hand and racing back to our house. She was fearless: she had always chosen the peanut-allergy table at school since a boy she liked sat there – the cafeteria version of

The Magic Mountain. Nickie's childhood like all dreams sharpened artificially into stray vignettes when I tried to conjure it, then faded away entirely. Now tall and long-limbed and inscrutable, she seemed more than ever like a sniper. I felt paralysed beside her and the love I had for her was less for this new spiky Nickie than the old spiky one, which was still inside her somewhere, though it was a matter of faith to think so. Surely that was why faith had been invented: to raise teenagers without dying. Although of course it was also why death was invented: to escape teenagers altogether. When, in the last few months, Nickie had 'stood her ground' in various rooms of the house, screaming at me abusively, I would begin mutely to disrobe, slowly lifting my shirt over my head so as not to see her, and only that would send her flying out of the room in disgust. Only nakedness was silencing, but at least something was.

'I can't believe Maria's wearing white,' said Nickie.

I shrugged. 'What colour should she wear?'

'Grey!' Nickie said immediately. 'To acknowledge having a brain! A little grey matter!'

'Actually, I saw something on PBS recently that said only the outer bark of the brain – and it does look like bark – is grey. Apparently the other half of the brain has a lot of white matter. For connectivity.'

Nickie snorted, as she often did when I uttered the letters *PBS*. 'Then she should wear grey in acknowledgement of having half a brain.'

I nodded. 'I get your point,' I said.

Guests were eating canapés on paper plates and having their pictures taken with the bride. Not so much with Maria's new groom, a boy named Hank, which was short not for Henry but for Johannes, and who was not wearing sunglasses like everyone else but was sort of squinting at Maria in pride and disbelief. Hank was also a musician, though he mostly repaired banjos and guitars, restrung and varnished them, and that was how he, Maria and Ian had all met.

Now the air was filled with the old-silver-jewellery smell of oncoming rain. I edged toward Ian, who was looking for the next song, idly strumming, trying not to watch his father eye Maria.

'Whatcha got? "I'll Be There"?' I asked cheerfully. I had always liked Ian. He had chosen Maria like a character, met her on a semester abroad and then come home already married to her – much to the marvelling of his dad. Ian loved Maria, and was always loyal to her, no matter what story she was in, but Maria was a narrative girl and the story had to be spellbinding or she lost interest in the main character, who was sometimes herself and sometimes not. She was destined to marry and marry and marry. Ian smiled and began to sing 'I Will Always Love You', sounding oddly like Bob Dylan but without the sneer.

I swayed. I stayed. I did not get in the way.

'You are a saint,' I said when he finished. He was a sweet boy, and when Nickie was little he had often come over and played soccer in the yard with her and Maria.

'Oh no, I'm just a deposed king of corn. She bought the farm. I mean, I sold it to her, and then she flipped it and bought this one instead.' He motioned toward the endless field beyond the tent, where the corn was midget and standing in mud, June not having been hot enough to evaporate the puddles. The tomatoes and marijuana would not do well this year. 'Last night I had a dream that I was in *West Side Story* and had forgotten all the words to "I like to be in America." Doesn't take a genius to figure that one out.'

'No,' I said. 'I guess not.'

'Jesus, what is my dad *doing*?' Ian said, looking down and away.

Ian's father was still prowling the perimeter, a little drunkenly, not taking his eyes off the bride.

'The older generation,' I said, shaking my head, as if it didn't include me. 'They can't take any change. There's too much missingness that has already accumulated. They can't take any more.'

'Geez,' Ian said, glancing up and over again. 'I wish my dad would just get over her.'

I swallowed more wine while holding Ian's lemonade. Over by the apple tree there were three squirrels. A threesome of squirrels looked ominous, like a plague. 'What other songs ya got?' I asked him. Nickie was off talking to Johannes Hank.

'I have to save a couple for the actual ceremony.'

'There's going to be an actual ceremony?'

'Sort of. Maybe not *actual* actual. They have things they want to recite to each other.'

'Oh yes, that,' I said.

'They're going to walk up together from this canopy toward the house, say whatever, and then people get to eat.' Everyone had brought food and it was spread out on a long table between the house and the barn. I had brought two large roaster chickens, cooked accidentally on Clean while I was listening to Michael Jackson on my iPod. But the chickens had looked OK, I thought: hanging off the bone a bit but otherwise fine, even if not as fine as when they had started and had been Amish and air-chilled and a fortune. When I had bought them the day before at Whole Foods and gasped at the total on my receipt, the cashier had said, 'Yes. Some people know how to shop here and some people don't.'

'Thirty-three thirty-three. Perhaps that's good luck.'

'Yup. It's about as lucky as two dead birds get to be,' said the cashier.

'Is there a priest or anything? Will the marriage be legal?' I now asked Ian.

Ian smiled and shrugged.

'They're going to say "You do" after the other one says "I do". Double indemnity.'

I put his lemonade down on a nearby table and gave him a soft chuck on the shoulder. We both looked across the yard at Hank, who was wearing a tie made of small yellow pop beads that formed themselves into the shape of an ear of corn. It had ingeniousness and tackiness both, like so much else created by people.

'That's a lot of *do*s.'

'I know. But I'm not making a beeline for the jokes.'

'The jokes?'

'The doozy one, the do-do one. I'm not going to make any of them.'

'Why would you make jokes? It's not like you're the best man.'

Ian looked down and twisted his mouth a little.

'Oh, dear. You *are*?' I said. I squinted at him. When young I had practised doing the upside-down wink of a bird.

'Don't ask,' he said.

'Hey, look.' I put my arm around him. 'George Harrison did it. And no one thought twice. Or, well, no one thought more than twice.'

Nickie approached me quickly from across the grass. 'Mom. Your chickens look disgusting. It's like they were hit by a truck.'

The wedding party had started to line up – except Ian, who had to play. They were going to get this ceremony over with quickly, before the storm clouds to the west drifted near and made things worse. The bridesmaids began stepping first, a short trajectory from the canopy to the rose bushes, where the *I do*s would be said. Ian played 'Here Comes the Bride'. The bridesmaids were in pastels: one the light peach of baby aspirin; one the seafoam green of low-dose clonazepam; the other the pale daffodil of the next lowest dose of clonazepam. What a good idea to have the look of Big Pharma at your wedding. Why hadn't I thought of that? Why hadn't I thought of that until now?

'I take thee, dear Maria . . .' They were uttering these promises themselves just as Ian said they would. Hank said, 'I do,' and Maria said, 'You do.' Then vice versa. At least Maria had taken off her sunglasses. *Young people*, I tried not to say out loud with a sigh. Time went slowly, then stood still, then became undetectable, so who knew how long all this was taking?

A loud noise like mechanized thunder was coming from the highway. Strangely, it was not a storm. A group of motorcyclists boomed up the road, and instead of roaring by us, slowed, then turned right in at the driveway, a dozen of them – all on Harleys. I didn't really know motorcycles, but I knew that every biker from Platteville to Manitowoc owned a Harley. That was just a regional fact. They switched off their engines. None of the riders wore a helmet – they wore bandannas – except for the leader, who wore a football helmet with some plush puppy ears which had been snipped from some child's stuffed animal then glued on either side. He took out a handgun and fired it three times into the air.

Several guests screamed. I could make no sound at all.

The biker with the gun and the puppy ears began to shout. 'I have a firearms licence and those were blanks and this is self-defence because our group here has an easement that extends just this far into this driveway. Also? We were abused as children and as adults and moreover we have been eating a hell of a lot of Twinkies. Also? We are actually very peaceful people. We just know that life can get quite startling in its switches of channels. That there is a river and sea figure of speech as well as a TV one. Which is why as life moves rudely past, you have to give it room. We understand that. An occasion like this means No More Forks in the Road. All mistakes are behind you, and that means it's no longer really possible to make one. Not a big one. You already done that. I need to speak first here to the bride.' He looked around, but no one moved. He cleared his throat a bit. 'The errors a person already made can step forward and announce themselves and then freeze themselves into a charming little sculpture garden that can no longer hurt you. Like a cemetery. And like a cemetery it is the kind of freedom that is the opposite of free.' He looked in a puzzled way across the property toward Maria. 'It's the flickering quantum zone of gun and none, got and not.' He shifted uncomfortably, as if the phrase 'flickering quantum zone' had taken a lot out of him. 'As I said, now I need to speak to the bride. Would that be you?'

Maria shouted at him in Portuguese. Her bridesmaids joined in.

'What are they saying?' I murmured to Nickie.

'I forgot all my Portuguese,' she said. 'My whole childhood I only remember Maria saying "good job" to everything I did, so I now think of that as Portuguese.'

'Yes,' I murmured. 'So do I.'

'Good job!' Nickie shouted belligerently at the biker. 'Good job being an asshole and interrupting a wedding!'

'Nickie, leave this to the grown-ups,' I whispered.

But the guests just stood there, paralysed, except Ian, who, seemingly very far off on the horizon, slowly stood, placing his guitar on the ground. He then took his white collapsible chair in both hands and raised it over his head.

'Are you Caitlin?' The puppy-eared biker continued to address Maria and she continued to curse, waving her sprigs of mint and spiraea at him. '*Vai embora, babaca!*' She gave him the finger, and when Hank tried to calm her, she gave Hank the finger. '*Foda-se!*'

The biker looked around with an expression that suggested he believed he might have the wrong country wedding. He took out his cellphone, took off his helmet, pressed someone on speed dial, then turned to speak into it. 'Yo! Joe. I don't think you gave me the right address . . . yeah . . . no, you don't get it. This ain't Caitlin's place . . . What? No, listen! What I'm saying is: wrong addressee! This ain't it. No speaky zee English here –' He slammed his phone shut. He put his helmet back on. But Ian was trotting slowly toward him with the chair over his head, crying the yelping cry of anyone who was trying to be a hero at his ex-wife's wedding.

'Sorry, people,' the biker said. He gave the approaching Ian only a quick unfazed double take. He flicked one of his puppy ears at him and hurried to straddle his bike. 'Wrong address, everybody!' Then his whole too-stoned-to-be-menacing gang started up their engines and rode away in a roar, kicking up dust from the driveway gravel. It was a relief to see them go. Ian continued to run down the road after them, howling, chair overhead, though the motorcycles were quickly out of sight.

'Should we follow Ian?' asked Nickie. Someone near us was phoning the police.

'Let Ian get it out of his system,' I said.

'Yeah,' she said and now made a beeline for Maria.

'Good job!' I could hear Nickie say to Maria. 'Good job getting married!' And then Nickie threw her arms around her former caretaker and began, hunched and heaving, to weep on her shoulder.

I couldn't bear to watch. There was a big black zigzag across my heart. I could hear Maria say, 'Tank you for combing, Nickie. You and your muzzer are my hairos.'

Ian had not returned and no one had gone looking for him. He would be back in time for the rain. There was a rent-a-disc-jockey who put on some music, which started to blare from the speakers. Michael Jackson again. Every day there was something new to mourn and something old to celebrate: civilization had learned this long ago and continued to remind us. Was that what the biker had meant? I moved toward the buffet table.

'You know, when you're hungry, there's nothing better than food,' I said to a perfect stranger. I cut a small chunk of ham. I placed a devilled egg in my mouth and resisted the temptation to position it in front of my teeth and smile scarily, the way we had as children. I chewed and swallowed and grabbed another one. Soon no doubt I would resemble a large vertical snake who had swallowed a rat. That rat Ben. Snakes would eat a sirloin steak only if it were disguised behind the head of a small rodent. There was a lesson somewhere in there and just a little more wine would reveal it.

'Oh, look at those sad chickens!' I said ambiguously and with my mouth full. There were rumours that the wedding cake was still being frosted and that it would take a while. A few people were starting to dance, before the dark clouds burst open and ruined everything. Next to the food table was a smaller one displaying a variety of insect repellents, aerosols and creams, as if it were the vanity corner of a posh ladies' room, except with discrete constellations of gnats. Guests were spraying themselves a little too close to the food, and the smells of citronella and imminent rain combined in the air.

The biker was right: you had to unfreeze your feet, take blind steps backward, risk a loss of balance, risk an endless fall, in order to give life room. Was that what he had said? Who knew? People were shaking their bodies to Michael Jackson's 'Shake your Body'. I wanted this song played at my funeral. Also the Doobie Brothers' 'Takin' It to the Streets'. Also 'Have Yourself a Merry Little Christmas' – just to fuck with people.

I put down my paper plate and plastic wine glass. I looked over at Ian's dad, who was once again brooding off by himself. 'Come dance with someone your own age!' I called to him, and because he did not say, 'That is so not going to happen,' I approached him from across the lawn. As I got closer I could see that since the days he would sometimes come to our house to pick up Maria and drive her home himself in the silver sports car of the recently single, he had had some eye work done: a lift to remove the puff and bloat; he would rather look startled and insane than look fifty-six. I grabbed his hands and reeled him around. 'Whoa,' he said with something like a smile, and he let go with one hand to raise it over his head and flutter it in a jokey jazz razzmatazz. In sign language it was the sign for applause. I needed my breath for dancing, so I tried not to laugh. Instead I fixed my face into a grin, and, ah, for a second the sun came out to light up the side of the red and spinning barn. ■

The Common Cold

To me she arrives this morning
dressed in some
man's homely, soft, cast-off
lover's shawl, and some
woman's memory of a third
grade teacher who loved
her students a little too much.
(Those warm
hugs that went
on and on and on.)

She puts her hand to my head
and says, 'Laura, you

should go back to bed.'

But I have lunches to pack, socks
on the floor, while the dust settles on
the *I've got to clean this pigsty up.*

(Rain at a bus stop.
Lingering kiss in a closet.)

And, tonight, I'm
the Athletic Booster mother
whether I feel like it or not, weakly

taking your dollar
from inside the concession stand:

I offer you your
caramel corn. (Birdsong
in a terrarium. Some
wavering distant
planet reflected
in a puddle.)

And as your dollars
pass between us
perhaps you will recall
how years ago we flirted
over some impossible
Cub Scout project.
Hammers

and saws, and seven
small boys tossing
humid marshmallows at each other.
And now those sons, taller

and faster than we are, are
poised on a line, ready
to run
at the firing of a gun.

But here we are again, you and I, the
two of us, tangled
up and biological. I've

forgotten your name, and
you never knew mine, but
in the morning you'll find
my damp kisses
all over your pillows,
my clammy flowers
blooming in your cellar,
my spring grass dewed
with mucus – and

you'll remember me
tonight in my
Go Dawgs T-shirt
standing at the centre
of the sweet clinging heat
of this concession stand
with my flushed cheeks, and
how, before
we touched, I
coughed into my hand.
Look:

Here we are
together
in bed all day again.

PLEASE TIM TICKLE LANA

Colin McAdam

GENERAL APPEARANCE & CONDITION:

(Normal)   Thin   ~~Obese~~
(Good)   Fair   Poor

DATE: ___7-1-96___

NO. _CN.454_ NAME: _Pepper_

SEX: _F_ AGE: _4_ LOCATION: _13_
IN BREEDING ( ) ON STUDY (X)

SIGNALMENT: _____

SKIN & HAIR: (Normal)

_____

ROUTINE (X)

TEETH: COMPLETE ( ) MISSING (→)

WEIGHT: (kg) _47.66_

3!2!1	2!1	1	2!1	1!2	1	1!2	1!2!3
-!-!-	-!-	-	-!-	-!-	-	-!-	-!-!-
-!-!-	-!-	-	-!-	-!-	-	-!-	-!-!-

R 3!2!1 2!1 1 2!1 1!2 1 1!2 1!2!3 L

LYMPH NODES:
Tonsilar _NP_
Submandibular _NP_
Cervical _NP_
Axillary _barely palpable L++?_
Inguinal (R) side (one) palpable

THORAX - AUSCULTATION: (Normal)

ABDOMEN - PALPATION: (Normal)

Spleen _NP_
Liver _NP_

LAB EVALUATION: (CBC) (Chemistries) Urine
Fecal   Other

GENITOURINARY: (Normal)
External _____
Internal _____

SPECIAL EXAMINATIONS: ECG X-Ray (TB)
Other

TREATMENT: _Ivomec SC_
(R) _Cerumen_

HEAD, TRUNK, ARMS, LEGS, HANDS & FEET: (Normal)

CLIN: _Cohn_ TECH: _TA_

COMMENT OR RECOMMENDATION:
Cage change

EYES, EARS, NOSE & THROAT: (Normal)

COURTESY COLIN McADAM

Spring in Canada can be an unconvincing season. In Montreal, where I used to live, the weather will suddenly turn warm, and the sun can seem like a youthful idiot shouting THERE'S HOPE, THERE'S HOPE to an audience of corpses. On a day like that, I drove to a place that changed my life.

I was approaching forty. I was madly in love. I was daily aware of the inadequacy of words to describe the joy and ache I felt, and at the same time I had no need for words. I went to a lousy therapist and told her how good I felt and she said she had heard the same from a number of men recently: adultery had done them good. I was in the middle of a divorce, and had done some truly shitty things to people I loved. My son was born in the midst of my failure to stay married. Regret had left bruises behind my eyes.

On that spring day when the sky was hot and the ground was dead, I found myself face-to-face with a chimpanzee named Spock. I had been reading about chimps for a couple of years. I was intrigued by the fact that we classify ourselves as great apes, and have more in common with chimpanzees, genetically, than chimpanzees have with gorillas, and yet rarely talk about ourselves, seriously, as apes.

I had begun writing a novel about chimps based on my book research, and found that I needed to meet some in the flesh. I wanted to know their movements, their sounds, their anger and their smell. I discovered a sanctuary that was less than a half-hour's drive from my apartment in Montreal. It was home to nineteen chimpanzees and various other animals rescued or retired from service to humans.

Spock was a little over thirty years old and weighed more than two hundred pounds. He approached with his hair on end, loping along a steel-enclosed catwalk. The co-founder of the sanctuary, Gloria, stopped near him and said, 'There's my Spock!' in a childish tone. At first it seemed as appropriate as saying 'Hey, little fella' to Genghis Khan. Spock had shoulders like boulders and homicidal eyes. He was the first adult chimp I had encountered so closely and I hadn't expected to feel such fear. His hands were massive and he seemed to embody most of the impulses that we legislate against. Without that steel fence I would have been his plaything. But when he heard Gloria's endearing voice he bobbed his head, softened and showed the face of a grandpa.

When I first started reading about chimpanzees I was attracted to the story of ape language studies: the fact that other apes could learn symbolic languages and communicate with us was moving to me. There was a chimp named Lana who lived in a room at Yerkes, a primate research centre in Atlanta, communicating with humans through a system of lexigrams called Yerkish.

She spent her infancy in that small room and for long stretches of time her only companion was the computer. She received physical contact with researchers when she demonstrated her comprehension of symbols or was able to create a grammatically correct sentence.

Her main interlocutor was Dr Timothy Gill, whom she knew as Tim. A typical sentence of hers would be PLEASE MACHINE GIVE COKE, where the MACHINE was the computer that dispensed various treats and also played movies and music. When Dr Gill was involved in observation, Lana would often want him in the room with her. PLEASE TIM TICKLE LANA.

Like most human children, Lana had an early understanding of the concept of NO. She could be chastened by it, when she saw it on the machine, but she could also use it to assert her own needs and disapproval. When one of the researchers drank Coke on the other side of the observation window and there was none available to Lana, she stamped her foot and hit the NO button. When Tim put a slice of banana in his mouth instead of in the dispenser for Lana, she hooted angrily, ran to the keyboard and said NO, NO, NO.

Lana knew the lexigrams for BOWL and CAN, and was learning the distinction between containers. Tim arrived one morning with a bowl, a can and a cardboard box. While Lana watched, he put an M&M candy in the box. Here is Lana learning the meaning of BOX.

Lana: ? TIM GIVE LANA THIS CAN.

Tim: YES. (Tim gives her the empty can, which she at once discards.)

Lana: ? TIM GIVE LANA THIS CAN.

Tim: NO CAN.

Lana: ? TIM GIVE LANA THIS BOWL.

Tim: YES. (Tim gives her the empty bowl.)

Lana: ? SHELLEY (sentence unfinished)

Tim: NO SHELLEY. (Shelley, another technician who worked with Lana, is not present.)

Lana: ? TIM GIVE LANA THIS BOWL. (Before Tim can answer, Lana goes on.)

Lana: ? TIM GIVE LANA NAME-OF THIS.

Tim: BOX NAME-OF THIS.

Lana: YES. (Short pause, and then) ? TIM GIVE LANA THIS BOX.

Tim: YES. (Tim gives it to her, she rips it open and eats the M&M.)

What I like about these transcripts is the childishness, the simplicity and familiar energy of a little girl wanting company and treats. I was charmed by chimpanzees and bonobos because they seemed so human. Over the years I have pondered the narcissism of that.

The one who charmed me the most in books was Washoe, the famous chimp who learned American Sign Language in the late 1960s. Roger Fouts wrote a wonderful memoir called *Next of Kin* about his relationship with Washoe – he was her teacher, student and friend. Here he is recounting one of their conversations in American Sign Language, where he uses upper-case letters to transcribe their signs:

> She once pestered me to let her try a cigarette I was smoking:
> GIVE ME SMOKE, WASHOE SMOKE, HURRY GIVE SMOKE. Finally
> I signed ASK POLITELY. She responded PLEASE GIVE ME THAT
> HOT SMOKE.

I love that she throws that word in: HOT. From a writer's perspective, adjectives are agents of persuasion, of surprise, of forcing a reader to look. Washoe uses her hands to give that smoke an urgent presence.

I found myself playing catch one day with a chimpanzee named Binky. We were throwing an apple back and forth – he was standing behind a fence inside his metal-and-concrete bedroom. Binky was in his late teens and was big. He scared the hair off me. The game went on until Binky dropped the fruit. As I bent down to pick it up Binky took a mouthful of water and drenched my face when I stood. He was agitated and gestured towards a bottle of Gatorade that was on the table behind me. As I absorbed the humiliation of having water spat in my face, I realized that what he had wanted all along was the bottle of Gatorade. The apple was his tool for making friends and getting my attention; it was like Washoe's talking hands. Once I gave him the Gatorade he threw the empty water bottle at my head.

I came to believe that what chimps do with hands and fingers, people do with their tongues. In human life words woo or sway, they provoke, inform and speak of an individual's perception. Our words help us find our place in a group, the words of others tell us whether they are one of us. If speaking and tool use come from the same place in the brain, then I thought of a word as a tool. A word is touch. It became a way for me to understand the physical origins of language, its physical effects. Instead of focusing on language as something that distinguished me as a human, I started thinking about words as fists and caresses, fingers grooming and soothing.

The sanctuary near Montreal was a thoughtfully designed place – all areas were built with chimps (and safety) as the main consideration. Each chimp had his or her own bedroom, with an elevated platform and places to nest as they might in the wild. There were indoor and outdoor play areas, and while the outdoor ones were lovely and spacious, the indoor areas were also large and varied; this was after all a suburb of Montreal and even rugged-up humans could not be comfortable outside for long. The indoor space had concrete floors, lounge areas and climbing apparatus. Some spaces had been divided into identical-looking parts because not all of the group got along with one another. There was a big kitchen at the centre of all the bedrooms, where a TV was often on, and where the days played out with the endless preparation of meals. The chimps had trolleys laden with food in front of each of their bedrooms, which they could reach through gaps in the latticed steel that sealed both chimp and human worlds.

I had read about the recognition and revulsion that people commonly feel when they first meet chimpanzees. Their company can force us to dispense with our fictions, and those who believe their own fictions too deeply are often disgusted by what looks like a parody of our behaviour, of our bodies. It was the time of the month for one of the females, Pepper. Her menstrual blood dripped like Kool-Aid from the folds of her swollen pudendum, and to call it a pudendum, with the word's implication of shyness, is to do that thing a disservice. It was as large, pink, arrogant and jowly as Winston Churchill's head.

What I immediately learned was that to have a generalized perception of the appearance of chimpanzees is a mistake. They are truly individuals, and understanding that so vividly was a step for me towards respecting them more deeply. Famous chimps like Lana are young, pale-faced and endearing. The common cultural perception of them is as little goofs, man-children. While touring my novel I have often been asked for photos of myself with one of them. Producers wonder if I might bring a chimp with me to radio interviews. I had known that chimps grew large, that their faces darkened, that they were violent and seven times stronger than human males, but to see these facts in the flesh was truly intimidating. They wouldn't sit quietly in a studio.

It wasn't just their size – not all were large. They had a presence that demanded all of my attention. I felt like I had entered a room of pickpockets who were honest about being pickpockets. These are our switchblades. I was always on the other side of a steel grid, but I rarely felt safe. Imagine walking into a bar in a small town where everyone is unfamiliar to you. Some are sizing you up, pondering your manner and the enemies you remind them of. Some are curious to meet you. You have no common language except the movement of your bodies. How do I present myself to creatures that don't know my language, that won't appreciate my irony and subterfuge? What am I when my words are not understood?

I talked to all of them in baby talk, and everyone who worked there did the same.

The individuals who were curious came close to the metal grid. They put their worn black fingers through the holes to reach out. I was warned not to touch them because the mischievous among them might hold onto my hand and not let go. They might break my fingers or bite them off – as had happened to others. It was nonetheless very hard not to reach out in return. Some gestured with the familiar inward wave of the hand, come here. They held their hands palm upward under the fence, tried to reach through it.

Several of them were HIV-positive. Fifteen of the original nineteen had come to the sanctuary from a biomedical lab in upstate New York called LEMSIP, the Laboratory for Experimental Medicine and Surgery in Primates, affiliated with New York University. The chimpanzees had been deliberately infected with various strains of HIV, hepatitis and other diseases. Chimps and humans can pass each other everything from polio and herpes to the common cold and flu. I signed a waiver stating I would make no claims against the sanctuary if I happened to be infected with something.

I was so keen to connect with them that it didn't give me pause. They spat in my face several times. Chimps in captivity will often spit, either to get your attention or to tell you to fuck off. I suppose their illnesses sharpened these already edgy exchanges for me.

Everything was heightened – fear, curiosity, the search for trust. Because many of them embodied such a coiled menace, the usual dynamic of joining a group – the awareness of judgement, the tension between welcome and rejection – felt exaggerated. I have rarely been so rationally aware of my insecurities. I had an unnerving sense that I was being watched, even by that one over there with her back turned. A male would suddenly arise with hair on end, stamp his foot and hoot, the group would be disturbed, the noise would be deafening and the air thereafter all the more electric. Even in moments of peace there was unease.

Pepper came towards me and we sat across from each other. I looked into her eyes and thought of the importance of eye contact in human life – strangers on a subway, how we know when someone is listening. I looked at her calmly and thought she was lovely. Her fingers were elegant. There was a light in her eyes. Her hand was outstretched to me under the fence and I wanted to hold it.

What I know about humans and human history is that we are empathetic, altruistic, imaginative and creative; we are social and our societies and families always contain some sort of hierarchy; we are miserable, depressive, murderous and greedy; we are afraid of strangers but sometimes make them welcome; we need and fear touch; there is politics to our food, politics to our mating, and meat is controversial; we make tools, and rely on others to pass on solutions; we share, beg, feel jealous, masturbate, care for others' children, kill and kidnap others' children, and we are judged for how we suffer and nurture our young.

All of this is documented chimpanzee behaviour. I came to the sanctuary already knowing, intellectually, that we were kin, but meeting Pepper made me feel it more deeply.

She was HIV-positive and had endured decades of biopsies and gunshot anaesthetics. As I heard some of the details of her life from Gloria, Pepper was sizing me up and urgently inviting me to touch her. She tried to groom a small freckle off my hand. I understood her grooming noises and gestures as a desire to get to know me, to help me.

When someone suffers torture and imprisonment, and comes out the other side to make friends with strangers, is this the apex of humanity, a triumph of will, or is it ape nature?

In my visits to this and other sanctuaries there were plenty of moments of strangeness and discomfort, times when I knew profoundly that I was not a chimpanzee. They are so loud, for one thing. Especially in rooms with concrete floors. I have an audio recording of myself presenting a bottle of Gatorade to an adult chimp named Regius. His pant-hoot starts like the breath of a scurrying dog and then rises and thickens, gathers a mood of fear and revelation and ends at a pitch of such violent joy that whenever I replay it I laugh and feel uncomfortable. At the time I remember thinking, Christ, Regius, it's only Gatorade.

Of course, that excessive joy and lack of shame are what can make them so attractive. There are many stories from the primatologists Frans de Waal and Jane Goodall about chimps practising deceit, creating a fictional disturbance to occupy a group in one place in order to get their hands on food somewhere else. I would never claim that they are what we would call innocent or honest. But their behaviour reminded me of how much we learn to dissemble in our own groups, and how refreshing it can be to encounter directness. Regius took a liking to my partner on one occasion; he lay on his back, spreadeagled, and invited her to touch his balls in a way that made me blush. I saw a middle-aged female named Sue Ellen savour a bowl of spaghetti with such Mardi Gras abandon that I cried and made it an important moment in my novel.

Perhaps knowing their histories made a difference. Months after my first visit I went through Pepper's medical file from LEMSIP.

Her blood work was sometimes processed by independent labs where the technicians did not know that she was a chimpanzee. Her cholesterol tests were set out identically to mine – the same range of normal. When her blood tested positive for HIV, the form from the lab declared that it was legally required for 'all test results [to] be relayed to the patient only by physicians or personnel suitably trained to counsel the individual as to the significance of the report'. Words from a caring physician that might soothe the human patient, words that might amount to a hand on the shoulder or a hug in the wake of bad news; words completely without meaning to a chimpanzee.

I read a number of scientific papers that emerged from this HIV research. The language was fascinating. Here is a sing-song description of a vaccine being prepared: 'The gp160-MN gene was placed under the transcriptional control of the H6 vaccinia virus promoter and then recombined into a canarypox virus. The resulting ALVAC-HIV vCP125 recombinant was amplified in specific-pathogen-free primary chicken embryo fibroblasts, lyophilized, and stored at 4 degrees Celsius until used.'

I puzzled through these papers and found clues of Pepper and her future friends at the sanctuary being the subjects of these experiments (the chimps were identified by numbers tattooed on their chests), and as I tried to understand the language I realized that these barely English descriptions were the sounds of a species trying to survive. When I learned more about these environments and trials, what a macabre and bloody harvest they amounted to, I saw these technical terms, these arcane clinicisms, as a means of doing dirty work and not having to look at it. The research was predicated by one sympathetic animal acknowledging the genetic and immunological kinship of another; yet it could only be conducted by ignoring most of that kinship. The diction makes it difficult to remember that there were living bodies involved.

The quote above was part of a study that took place over five years. What this meant for Pepper and the others was thousands of days and nights in a cage, hundreds of knock-downs, infections and a solitary, relentless battle with disease. Pepper was in those cages for almost thirty years.

Having read so much about chimpanzees I had to adjust to them as animals when I met them, as flesh and blood rather than abstractions. Study after study presents them as embodiments of data: they are sensitive communicators; they remember sequences of numbers; they get depressed in middle age. The data are often wonderful and telling, but they somehow collect in a corner – that place we look when we are searching for random facts and cute coincidences, those moments when the 'natural' world might amusingly reflect our own. The further we get from having to find our own food, the less awareness we have of our nature. Understanding these individuals at the sanctuary as animals meant adjusting to myself as an animal. I was not finding an ape within. I was realizing that the whole of me is an ape, that our genes, our biology, our behaviour in groups are not just coincidentally related to other apes but inescapable facts that I arise and go to sleep to. That I dream with.

We all embody a range of contradictions. Chimpanzees and humans hate to see injuries, and cause them all the time. Chimps and humans choose their factions, betray their friends and use enemies to consolidate friendships. While I hate the violence that humans have inflicted on chimps, I've seen chilling and deplorable fights between chimps themselves – capricious acts of bullying and murder which show that they can have as much disdain for life and kin as we can.

I have had this ambition to find a language for the ape reality of days. Alpha chimps, according to Frans de Waal, can engender such respect that other chimps will bow to their sleeping bodies. That image has stayed with me, and made me think that an alpha, in ape societies, is one who controls conscience. When a male chimpanzee wishes to eat someone else's fruit or have a dalliance with an attractive female, he will go to a sleeping alpha and bow. A contrite sinner kneeling before a priest. Clearly the alpha is present in his mind as he negotiates his desires. To me, this is why various godheads have so successfully brought people together through human history – it is natural for apes to look for an arbitrator to govern individual desires, and natural for us to think of others who may or may not be present as we step forth and make our mistakes.

The alpha is part of a dynamic of dominance and submission that plays out constantly in our lives. When my three-year-old daughter wants something, she will sometimes ask me first. I can see fibs and deceit beginning to bloom in her pupils like tiny black dahlias, and I lie to her regularly to get what I want. If she makes a mess or hurts herself she will come to me for comfort or to apologize if her mother isn't around, and if we are all together she treats me like dirt. She is my alpha as much as I am hers. I find it helpful to think of an alpha as a real or imagined force greater than myself that I may or may not bow to as I go through my days: a voice or force to be considered. My father, partner, editors, ex-wife and bankers have all been my alphas – people I have needed to please whose voices have occasionally checked my actions, and my desires. This is basic ape behaviour, human behaviour.

I no longer see human beings as I used to. I get frustrated that we have a limited language for the very nature that gives us language, no way of calling ourselves 'apes' without inducing giggles or indignation. Part of the ape reality of my days is that I often forget I am one. Trying to remember it has sometimes left me lonely.

I like watching hockey. When I see crowds cheering and hooting, egging on fights and deploring them when someone is seriously injured, I think: apes. I look at my competitive side, my need for friends, my wish to be heard, and I think: ape. Ethnic conflicts and superpowers rattling sabres: apes. Debates over immigration. Mothers supporting other women and biting the backs of rivals. I think of magazines and newspapers as grooming sessions, gatherings of the like-minded who use words and idioms like handclasps, each contributor wanting to steer the group towards his or her perspective. It might sound reductive to some people, but it has been a comforting way of understanding my life.

I left my wife shortly after she gave birth. The trauma of that changed me, and my family, forever. I know that when I watched my son's birth, my mind in a despicable mess, he came out gold and wet and I had two clear thoughts: I am proud of him already; and, how can we have witnessed the spectacle of birth so many billions of times and yet believe we are separate from animals?

Lana, the joyful, curious chimpanzee who learned how to use the computer to talk to Tim, ended up being kept in the lab at Yerkes and became part of the breeding programme. I recently met a woman who worked with her on that original language study. She had returned to Yerkes and met Lana again, forty years later. She said that Lana clearly remembered her. Lana had had several kids at Yerkes, all of them taken away from her for various studies. The woman said that Lana's eyes were distant, and sad.

I cherish my partner's eyes, and she accepts the fact that I think of her as an ape. Our daughter draws us to the playground. She plays in the sandbox and tries to take toys from other kids, cries when they are taken from her. The adults arbitrate, teach the kids how to share. When the kids are upset we all say 'use your words'. Over there some women are talking about something serious; they are making it clear that they are friends and that I am not welcome to join their conversation. The men near the swings stand with folded arms and talk about their work, occasionally making eye contact with each other. One of them says he has learned to hustle more since he became a father, doesn't worry about rejection so much and doesn't get angry when people don't like what he's selling. He's getting along better with everyone and his bank account shows it. His kids are tumbling, fighting and playing. My daughter is particularly good at the monkey bars. I'm hungry, and irritable because of it, and I will probably wake up in the night in some kind of panic, or my partner will, my daughter definitely will; all of us scared of the things we can't see. People at the playground say goodnight, we all go home to eat, to read stories and watch TV, forget ourselves on the couch. ■

NUDITY

Norman Rush

Norman Rush, April 1949
Courtesy of the author

From an early age, I was very interested in nudity. My father was a nudist manqué. He made many attempts, which I was witness to, to cajole my mother into going with him to a genuine nudist colony in Mendocino County. There was considerable casual nudity exhibited by both my parents in the normal processes of dressing and bathing and sunbathing au naturel on the veranda of our summer place near Monte Rio, where there was sufficient privacy, in their opinion. Whether my younger brother and I were to be included in the proposed nudist colony expeditions was never made clear. My mother didn't go for it and I suspect didn't discuss Dad's importunings with anyone, even her sisters. My father subscribed to *Sunshine and Health*, the premier nudist magazine, which my brother and I also read faithfully. Our home in post-war, middle-class East Oakland was a fort-like, solid, voluminous house originally built by a general contractor for his own family. It was across the street from a semi-castle owned by Frank Epperson, the inventor of the Popsicle. Mrs Epperson told my mother, who told everyone, that in her view, sex was sinful even in marriage except when necessary for procreation. To endure the conception of their four children, Mrs Epperson had, she revealed (recommending it to my mother), prepared for each obligatory act by consuming large quantities of aspirin. The medieval sexual narrowness of Mrs Epperson was a subject of scornful dinner-table discussion. Nudity was on my mind rather a lot. I was about nine at this time. The nudity of my parents did not assuage my ripening interest, but rather inflamed it. I wanted to see other naked female humans, and I wanted my father to keep his bathrobe on.

In the fourth or fifth grade at Horace Mann Elementary School I was the leader of a band of boys who, at recess, charged around the schoolyard in flying wedge formation. We would target clusters of girls and run at them shouting, 'Hey, hey, ho, ho, let's all go to the Burless Show.' I knew vaguely that these shows involved, in some way, naked ladies. I knew this because when my rather slow-moving old grandfather was visiting us, my father seized any opportunity he could to take him downtown to one of the Roxie Theater's regular 'burless' programmes. This was ostensibly to cheer the dear old fellow up. My grandfather showed enthusiasm for this diversion, in particular for a show called 'Strip Strip Hooray'. My mother disapproved of these excursions, and eventually ended them. It's true that they had gotten rather frequent. If my mother seems unduly regulatory, it has, in fairness, to be kept in mind that my father had married her only after a démarche by the two potential grandmothers. My mother was three months pregnant (with me), and my father, believing he'd had a mere interlude, had relocated to Los Angeles from San Francisco on urgent business for the Socialist Party. He was brought home in chains, as my mother bitterly expressed it, and the upshot was that no punishment she meted out for the rest of his life could ever outweigh her early humiliation. When she got mad at my father, we children (there would be five, altogether) were reminded that he'd fought marriage up to the last minute despite her pregnancy.

I nursed a precocious rage at the stratagems society was employing to keep me from seeing naked women. Perusing the cheesecake magazine collection of a boy named Mosca, whom we called The Fly, became the chief night-time activity on Cub Scout camping trips to Livermore and other nearby wastelands. The magazines were disappointing. I could see no reason why nipples, which I knew were mere outward valves, had to be covered up with pasties or the limbs of trees. Similarly with the pudendum. Why could one never see something as innocent as the escutcheon, whose function had to be to provide a modest veiling for the introitus?

My junior high Social Studies class provided some near-nudity.

It was run by Mr Planer, a jaded teacher with an Olympian attitude who regarded his students as hopeless brutes. He would allow us to vote, when class-work had been completed and there was time left over, for which one of the few available brief documentary films we would like to see again. The boys voted en bloc every time, while the girls' votes were split among a number of short subjects including *Wood Pulp to Paper*, *The Bessemer Converter* and *Flax*. The boys always chose the film in the canister labelled *Anthropology*. This documentary, with which many readers may be familiar from their exposure to the National Geographic Channel, featured bare-breasted women wearing only token skirts, and men wearing no clothing except extremely long, tapered gourds housing their penises. We boys called them 'dick guards'. When the women were on-screen there was utter silence in the classroom and when the men took centre stage there was raucous laughter from the boys and appalled silence from the girls. They thought it was 'dirty'. I don't know why Mr Planer enabled this over and over again.

My pursuit of the unrestricted gaze met continuing obstacles. On a rare visit to my Uncle Ralph's house, I managed, late one night, to introduce my older twin cousins (they had recently reached puberty), one female, to the game of strip poker. I did not actually know how to play this game, but improvised some rules that would get Renée's clothes off with the utmost possible speed. Unfortunately, her mother came looking for her while Renée was still in her underwear. Worse, my four-years-younger brother, always something of a saboteur when it came to any interest of mine, broke the furtive protocol we both had been observing re perusing *Sunshine and Health*. My father's backfile was kept in a drawer in his nightstand. Robert would regularly ascertain where my mother was in the house, and I would dash in and check the graphics out. One morning, however, he wandered out into the breakfast nook with a faux-beatific look on his face, ostentatiously holding up and reading a back issue of *Sunshine and Health*. My father was not present. My mother was taken aback and questioned him severely. He, affecting surprise, defended his choice of reading matter. 'It has good poetry in it, Ma!' he said. He then read out loud, with a sort of aesthetic piety, the following: 'Oh how I love to sleep out in the nude / Wake up in the morning feeling gude.' She swatted the magazine from his hand, and another corridor for my swelling interest collapsed before my eyes.

My closest childhood friend, Jack, worked as a stock boy at the Frances Shop, a fashion emporium on East 14th Street. While rolling up the awning, he lost control of the crank, which hit him in the jaw, disabling him for a couple of weeks. He induced me to take the job as his replacement, which paid very low wages, with the guarantee that, with the right timing, I could inch my head up over the back partition of the changing cubicles and get glimpses of flesh. I tried this once, standing on Jack's improvised platform, and did catch a woman in her bra and step-ins (which is what panties were called in those days), but I was terrified, and seeing underwear was in any case not my quest.

This account concludes even more shamefully. I apologize symbolically, sincerely and pointlessly, here, to both of my victims below. The wife of my father's best friend had been suddenly widowed. Her husband and her youngest child drowned in a swimming accident in the Eel River. C. came to us occasionally for consolation in the aftermath of her tragedy, and stayed for a few days each time. She would get my room and I would bunk with Robert. An arm of the attic ran behind the wall of my room against which the head of my bed was set. With infinite care, I drilled a peephole in the wall just behind the right-hand bedpost and well enough obscured by its serpentine carving. Twice I crept to my peephole, and, on the second and last essay, succeeded in securing a flash view of the widow's breasts. I hated myself. I plugged the hole with spackle. But this was only the penultimate cessation of my voyeurism. My mother hired M., an unmarried black woman who came with us from Oakland for the whole summer to help with all the kids, cousins included, in the family's rambling, crumbling place (it had come with a name, Azulikit – 'as you like it') in the Russian River country. M. was heftily built. In the room that became hers, I knew, the ancient window shade was a tattered thing with a triangular tear in a lower corner. One summer, I stationed myself on the outdoor walkway by M.'s room at the time of night when she would be preparing for bed. I was given a view of her body. M. had been grievously scarred, presumably in some fire calamity, across her entire chest and side. C. and M., both objects of my visual exploitation, had an absolute right to the privacy afforded by clothing. I understood it. These are true stories. The final two experiences sobered me into patience. ■

Cooley High
1991

I guess it's a funny thing, really,
    how I can't hear Boyz II Men,
even the 90s bedroom countdown
    and the colour blue of Michael McCrary's
'Injection, fellas' without wanting
    to cry. A real cry. Look! I've slipped into
the surprise and trapdoor
    of my own heartache
just like that. *The Cooleyhighharmony*
    on repeat in the tapedeck
as my mom and I drove up
    to boarding school, my first year. 1991.
And though I've tried, I can't stop being touched
    by the borrowed car, my mother's hands,
the steering wheel a kind of clock
    we moved with toward the finish line. We rode,
a slow unfurling of ourselves across
    a hundred twenty miles, despite history,
despite warnings of coloured kids
    washed by books, or kerosene and lye
in the white yards of schools
    far from their fathers
and the stars. And still, hundreds of us
    tumbling out of our houses
to be half-raised. The ghosts of children
    from the Perris Indian School

did come down from the hills, all the way
    from Riverside, to watch the odd quiet
of our take-leavings. Their hairs thick
    with cactus and grave dirt. The prickly pears
of their mouths warning, *Some parts of you will*
    die there. I can still see it all
so clearly now. The school gate is—a carving knife.
    This is
the future Mom chooses for me
    and she drives me to
my dormitory, room
    different from the one I woke in
beside my cousin and small sister, brother
    sleeping in the trundle. I have been thrown
into new orbit. This is
    an old story.   Distance
in the name of opportunity.
    The complicated sacrifice,
and so on.
    But I could have stayed home
for so long. With my people.
    Helped around the house. Gotten a job.
In Chicago, my mother's hometown,
    the death toll climbs like a serpent up the red graph.
We are 2,000 miles away, but the deaths of black
    kids everywhere are at her neck. So this is what
she chooses for me. I am not
    gifted, no more than Angel or Sargeant or LeNara
or most anybody, really,
    but know how to read and to obey the rules

of tests, and the academic officer
   says 'hope' and 'promise'
to my mother whose
   own mother would not choose my mother who
turns her back, suddenly the car (with her hands)
   is leaving. I think, Who will be
my parent now? as the orange trees
   dot the coming darkness
with their small fires, and not far
   the sadness of oaks and dry brush. Still,
the car (with her hands) leaving.
   Please stay with me as I
replay the last touch. My face
   buried in her hair and neck. How
I am quiet, and let her say
   'This is the best thing'
though I disbelieve it, even now.

   She was my mother, after all,
   and president of nothing.

DANGEROUS

Joy Williams

A year after my mother moved further out, she became obsessed with building a tortoise enclosure. This was in preparation for receiving a desert tortoise – *Gopherus agassizii* – or as the Indians would say, or rather had said, *komik'c-ed* – shell with living thing inside. That's the Tohono O'odham Indians. My mother said she'd read that somewhere.

I was recently at a party and found myself talking to a linguist and he told me that we had been pronouncing *komik'c-ed* incorrectly but that it meant pretty much what my mother claimed it meant.

Sometimes I drink too much but mostly I don't. I go to AA meetings on occasion but I don't really bond with those people, I don't see them socially. They're nice enough but some of them have been sober for twenty-five or thirty years. I have a copy of the Big Book and sometimes I read around in it but it never makes me cry like Wordsworth's *Preludes*, say. I don't have the *Preludes* any more. I misplaced it, unbelievable, but it was falling apart with my looking at it so much and I moved away too after my father died so it was probably misplaced then. My mother is a widow now for two years but she never worries about her situation or talks about it like some people would. She never let on to me or others that she was sorrowful or lonely. I'm twenty-one. It could be argued that there are worse ages to lose your father than in your nineteenth year but I found it to be a difficult time, mostly because I was just old enough to try to take it in stride. Sometimes I think it would have been worse if I was eight or even twelve and I don't know why I indulge myself like that. It doesn't make me feel better and I admit I have no imaginative access to the person I was when I was eight or twelve. I can't imagine this girl at all. I can't imagine having a conversation with her. My mother told me that when I was eight all I wanted to do was swim. Swim, swim, swim. Then I stopped wanting to do this. When I was twelve she said that my most cherished possession was a communication badge I'd earned in Girl Scouts. It showed a tower emitting wiggly lines.

Which is odd because communicating is not a skill I naturally or unnaturally possess. I'd prefer to think of myself as a witness, but honestly, I doubt I'm even that.

The apartment I moved into is a shithole but convenient. Bars, restaurants, automobile services galore and a Trader Joe's where you can buy pizzas fast-frozen in Italy and coconut water from Thailand, not that that's unusual any more, it's what's come to be expected. The apartment complex is clean, inexpensive and devoid of character. We tenants just refer to it as a shithole because it's so soul-sucking. We don't really believe our souls are being destroyed of course because we feel we have more power over our situation than that. The facility has a good view of sunsets in the summer when they're not at their most legendary and it's too hot to sit outside and view them anyway.

Shortly after my father died and I moved into the shithole without even my *Preludes* to remind me of loftier, simpler and more beautiful emotions, my mother sold our house in the foothills and moved into a run-down adobe on thirty acres of land in the mountains. Is there any kind of adobe other than run-down? I think not.

After a while she began to speak frequently of a neighbour, Willie, and his water-harvesting system. He had a 26,000-gallon below-ground cistern and got all his water from roof run-off during our infrequent but intense rains. I feared Willie might be a transitional figure in my mother's life but he turned out to be an old man in a wheelchair with an old wife so cheerful she had to have been on a serious drug regimen. They did have an ingenious water-collection system and I was given a tour of all the tanks and tubes and purifiers and washers and chambers that provided them with such good water and made them happy. They also kept bees and had an obese cat. The cat, or rather its alarming weight, seemed out of character for their way of life but I didn't mention it. Instead, I asked them if his name was spelled with an *e-w* or an *o-u*. They found this wildly amusing and later told my mother that they'd liked me very much. That and a dollar fifty will get me an organic peach, I said. I don't know why my mother's enthusiasm for them irritated me so much. Soon they were gone, however, both carried off by some pulmonary infection one gets from mouse pee. A man my mother described as a survivalist later moved into their house and I was told little concerning him other than he didn't seem to know how to keep the system going and ended up digging a well.

It was Lewis with an *e-w* that kept bringing diseased rodents into the house is my suspicion.

From the time I was ambulatory until I was fourteen when I refused to participate, every year on my birthday my father would video me going around an immense organ-pipe cactus in the city's botanical garden. The cactus is practically under lock and key now. It could never survive elsewhere certainly. Some miscreant would shoot it full of arrows or smack holes in it with a golf club.

My father would splice the frames and speed them up so that I would start off on my circuit, disappear for a moment and emerge a year older, again and again a year older, taller and less remarkable. I began as a skipping and smiling creature and gradually emerged as a slouching and scowling one. Still, my parents appeared unaware of the little film's existential horror. My mother claims that she no longer has it, that it no longer exists, and I have chosen to believe her.

On the other hand I find it difficult to believe that my father no longer exists. He lives in something I do not recognize. Or no longer recognize and will never again recognize. There are philosophers who maintain we are not our thoughts and that we should disassociate ourselves from them at every opportunity. But without this thought, I would have no experience of the world and even less knowledge of my heart.

I've had a comfortable life. I've not been troubled or found myself an outcast or disadvantaged in any way. This too was the case with my mother and father. Lives such as ours are no longer in vogue.

Since I've lived in the shithole, however, I've found that another's perception of me can sometimes be unexpected. For example, the other night I was looking at some jewellery in an unsecured case at Hacienda del Sol, waiting for my friends to arrive so that we could start drinking overpriced tamarind margaritas, and this hostess stalks up to me and says *can I help you* . . . in other words, you look beyond suspicious, what are you even doing here . . .

She appeared a somewhat older version of one of the paramedics who arrived at the house the night my father died, though it was unlikely that anyone would go from being a paramedic to an employee at a resort that had seen better days and was, in fact, in foreclosure. Though perhaps she had accumulated a record of not saving anyone and had lost her position as an emergency responder.

Do I know you? I asked. Or maybe it was, Have I seen you before? because I had never known her, even if she'd been the one to feel my father's last breath leave his body. She threw me a dismissive look and returned to her station to greet and seat a party of four, a party she'd evidently been expecting as they had planned ahead and had a reservation.

My point is that however fortunate your life or – considering the myriad grotesque ways one can depart from it – your death, it's usually strangers who have their hands on you at the end and usher you down the darkened aisle. Or rather that was one of my reflections as I waited for my friends with whom I would commence a night of drinking.

So my mother is out there alone, in what I swear is one of the darkest parts of the mountain, with only a rarely-in-residence survivalist for a neighbour, and she is erecting a 300-square-foot protective enclosure for a reptile that isn't even endangered, though my mother claims it should be.

I don't go out there much to visit, not nearly as often as I should, I suppose, but I'm aware that the work is proceeding slowly. My mother is insisting on doing everything herself. The most strenuous part is digging the trench, which Fish and Wildlife guidelines require to be fourteen inches deep. The trench is then to be filled with cement and a wall no less than three feet tall built upon it. All this is to prevent the tortoise from escaping, for this is to be an adopted tortoise, one displaced by development, and one that should not be allowed to return to an environment that is no longer hospitable to it. At the same time, everything within the enclosure should mimic its natural situation. There should be flowering trees and grasses, a water source and the beginnings of burrow excavations, facing both the north and the south, that the tortoise can complete.

The site my mother had chosen was several hundred yards from the adobe. Wouldn't it be easier, I asked, if she just enclosed an area using one of the house's walls? Then she wouldn't have to dig so much, it would be more of a garden, she could bring out a table and chairs, have her coffee out there in the morning, maybe have a little fire pit for the evening, no, not a fire pit certainly, what was I thinking, but possibly her aim should be the creation of a pleasant and meditative place that she could utilize for herself as well as for this yet unacquired tortoise.

Actually, I think a space for meditation is the last thing my mother needs. I don't know why I mentioned it. She didn't respond to my suggestion anyway. She simply said she was not doing this for herself.

The earth on the mountain is volcanic and poor. Some of the stones my mother dislodges are as big as medicine balls. She uses some sort of levering tool. Still, it's dangerous work as is every part of the grieving process if it's done correctly. Don't think I don't realize what my mother is up to.

If you injure yourself your independent ageing days might as well be over, I said. She laughed, which I hoped she would. Where did you come across that dreadful phrase, she asked. Someone in the shithole, I said, and she laughed again. Why are you punishing yourself, she said, by living in that place?

One of my acquaintances there is a widow too but she's only ten years older than I am. Her husband died in one of those stupid head-on wrecks blamed by the surviving driver on the setting sun.

It blinded me! She kept his shoes. People would visit her and there would be his running shoes in the bathroom, his boots by the couch, if he'd been old enough for slippers they would have certainly been by the bed. This was in their home before she moved here, sort of on display, she told me, sort of stagey. Everyone who saw them was moved to tears and she kept them out longer than she should have, she realized that. Then one day she just threw them away – they were too beat-up to give to charity – and she got rid of a lot of other things as well and moved into the shithole.

We can't keep pets here. It's one of the rules and is strictly enforced. No one cares. I mean no one tries to smuggle a pet in. They don't feel the lease violates their rights. Several years ago there was a tenant with a Great Dane who went off one morning and shot up his nursing class at the university because he'd received a bad assessment, killing his instructor and two fellow students before killing himself. There was not one mention of what happened to the dog afterwards, not a single mention. Information about the dog is unavailable to this day. I sometimes think of this guy who wanted to be certified as a nurse, and not only what was he thinking when he set off that morning to murder those people but what was he thinking leaving the dog behind with its dog toys and dog dishes and dog bed? What did he think was going to happen?

Tortoises spend half their life in burrows, from October into April. Should you see a tortoise outside its burrow in the winter months it's not well and veterinary assistance should be sought.

So, I say to my mother, have you met this tortoise?

She said she had not, but she had filled out all the paperwork and was on a list. She'd be contacted when the enclosure was complete.

So you don't know how old it is or whether it's a he or a she or whether it's a special-needs tortoise with a malformed shell or a missing leg.

I don't, my mother said.

I would think that after going through all of this, all the woman-hours and expense, you'd want a perfect tortoise.

Well, my mother said, maybe I'll get one.

My mother used to be much more talkative. There used to be a lot more going on, more being said, lots of cheerful filler. Maybe that's why I go to AA as much as I do because at least people are telling stories, pathetic and predictable as they may be, and all manner of reassurances and promises are being made. When I go into my mother's little house now, I don't recognize much. There seems to be very little remaining of the life I had known, been cocooned in, you might say. I should have emerged from it in glorious certitude by now.

Often I think, and it is with a certain dismay, that I will age out of the shithole one day, for it is a young crowd who reside here briefly and then move on. The ones who stay do not remain in touch with the ones who leave. What would we speak of with one another? When someone vacates, the manager comes in, paints the walls, sands the floors and cleans the windows. New tenants arrive quickly – it's cheap, practically free! It's convenient! We're not crazy about them at first but we gradually enfold them. No point in playing favourites here. We're all pretty much the same.

My mother finally finished the trench. It was pretty impressive when you think it was all accomplished by her hand. Then she bought some rebar and a cement mixer and in no time really it was all filled in and ready to accept the blocks. But then matters slowed down again. It was June and the heat was beginning to build. She'd be working, covered head to toe and with a hat and welder's gloves, but gradually she'd only get a few hours in between dawn and dusk. The rest of the time I don't know what she did – waited in that little adobe for dawn and dusk, I suppose. She didn't have air conditioning, there was just a rattling, inefficient swamp cooler in need of new pads.

What she's doing doesn't sound healthy, the young widow in the shithole said. You should take her out to dinner or something. Get her out of there. Insist upon it. Or she should take up running. I should take up running, I know. And what kind of a companion is a tortoise going to be? You're not even supposed to pick them up much are you?

Fish and Wildlife claim they're very personable, I said.

Those people are morons. Didn't they want to open a hunting season on sandhill cranes?

I don't know, I said.

You've probably never seen one but I'm from Colorado so I have. They're so elegant and they have this elaborate dance they do. They mate for life. Now there's loneliness when one's taken, there's real loneliness.

She can be pretty intense at times but she can be superficial too as with those shoes which I have the grace not to mention.

Certainly my mother did not need to be taken out to dinner. People aren't much help to one another under most circumstances is what I've found. I'm reminded of the evening I dropped in at AA and a ruddy-faced woman came up to me and said, I hear you've lost your mother, I'm so sorry. And I said, no, it was my father who died. And she said, oh, I'd heard it was your mother.

And that was it.

It was the Fourth of July when I managed to get out to my mother's house again. The blocks had been cemented in place and were ready to be plastered and my mother had found a gate that she'd installed and painted blue. It swung inside, though, rather than outside, which I found somewhat awkward.

We were in the kitchen of the adobe eating toasted bread and some cold soup my mother had made. I had brought a bottle of wine but my mother incredibly did not have a corkscrew. You could barely see the enclosure from the house. It was so strange to me that she would not want to be closer to it when it was finished and had its occupier, though to be truthful I could not imagine the creature inside very well or the relief that seeing it would provide.

Mom, I said.

I'm good, my mother said.

Her face was sun-darkened and her thinning hair looked as though it would be crisp to the touch.

Do you ever think of heaven? she asked.

No.

Good, she laughed. I don't want you thinking of heaven.

We never did, did we?

I wished I were twelve again and could ask questions and pretend the answers were what I needed.

How about divinity? she asked.

Gosh no, I said, that's even harder to think about, isn't it?

She said the exciting work was about to begin – the preparation of the inner keep.

Is that what it's called? I wondered, and she said that was what she called it.

I managed to get the cork out with a screwdriver. It seemed to take me forever. My mother accepted a glass of wine without comment and we resumed talking about the plants she would put in that would provide food and shade for the tortoise. I wondered what she would do when everything was complete and it was very close to being complete. Grief is dangerous work, I thought again, but when you have overcome it and it passes away, are you not left more bewildered and defenceless than ever?

I did not know what she meant by divinity but the strange word was not mentioned again.

Your mother is trying to contain her grief in a beautiful garden of her own devising, the young widow said. Or maybe it's not grief at all. Maybe it's something else, early onset something else. I'm sorry, she said, I don't mean to simplify your mother's situation in any way. Or yours. Or even mine, for that matter. You know what grief hates? Analysis or comfort of any kind.

I believed she was wrong. Grief thrives on comfort. Comfort is the vehicle by which it can go anywhere, inhabit anything. Still, I said, what does it love then?

The ones for which we grieve, she said. The lost. Grief knows how to love them because we don't know how to do it any more.

That's not true, I said.

Take Larry's shoes for example. What did I think I was doing?
I didn't know what I was doing.

They say there are many ways to grieve, I said. There's no one
right way to do it.

I could not help but speak falsely to her, I don't know why.

She sighed and shook her head. The skin around her mouth was
broken out in tiny pimples but her hair was pretty, dark and glossy like
a healthy animal's. She seemed younger than me, impossibly young,
and I did not want to discuss matters with her any more. She did not
drink which made my avoidance of her easier but I was left with her
perception of grief. I began to think of it as something substantial
and assured and apart, more competent and attentive than I, and no
longer mindful of me and my poor efforts.

I then began to fear that my mother would be denied the very
thing she had so inexplicably sought after my father's death. She
would never receive *komik'c-ed*. The programme would have closed
down. Even from the little I'd been told, the arrangement seemed
unwieldy and misguided. The tortoise had to be microchipped and
someone in an official capacity had to check on its health twice a year.
There weren't the public funds available for such things.

Instead, it turned out that my mother had not built the home
for the as-yet-unrealized tortoise on her land. A real estate agent
came out to see if the adjacent area would appraise out to make it
worthwhile to subdivide and noted the error. The enclosure was well
within her client's property line and had to be removed.

Appraised out, my mother said. Who comes up with these dreadful
phrases . . .

I agreed that language was becoming uglier the more it was
becoming irrelevant to our needs.

My mother took on the task of dismantling everything she had
accomplished. She broke up the walls and trucked away the rubble.
She even dug out the filled trench. Then she rough-raked the ground
and rolled some of the large stones back into place. She left the few
flowering shrubs and grasses she had so recently planted but without

protection the birds and animals that are so seldom seen quickly consumed them. Such is their need.

Eventually I moved out of the shithole, though I still go to AA. I've even stopped drinking. I would say then that all is continuing here. Is it the same way there? ■

Ghost Moth by *Michèle Forbes*

Northern Ireland, 1949. Katherine must choose between George Bedford – solid, reliable, devoted George – and Tom McKinley, who makes her feel alive. The reverberations of that summer – the passions spilled, the lies told and the bargains made – still clamour to be heard twenty years later.

'Beautifully written' Roddy Doyle

'A stellar debut' Sebastian Barry

Weidenfeld & Nicolson £12.99 | **HB**

Ambit

Ambit, founded in 1959 by Dr Martin Bax, is alive and kicking. Under new editorship and now in full colour it remains a place where you can delight in the company of old favourites and discover emerging writers and artists. Poetry, prose, flash fiction and art in an A5 quarterly.

Ambit £29.99 for a UK subscription, £9.99 for a single copy.

Subscribe now at ambitmagazine.co.uk

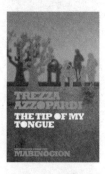

The Tip of My Tongue by *Trezza Azzopardi*

In this retelling of Geraint and Enid from the Celtic myth cycle the *Mabinogion*, Trezza Azzopardi transforms a medieval heroine who won't be silenced into a brave 1970s girl from downtown Splott in Cardiff who, no matter how difficult the circumstances, always seems to get the last word. Part of the series New Stories from the Mabinogion, masterly reworkings of traditional Welsh tales by contemporary writers.

Seren Books £8.99 | **PB**

The Dig by *Cynan Jones*

From a rising star of British fiction, *The Dig* is a powerful story of two lives violently intertwined that crackles with the raw energy of truly vital storytelling.

'Moving, evocative and utterly compelling' Jon McGregor

'Absolutely magnetic' Sarah Waters

Granta Books £12.99 | **HB**

THE EMILY DICKINSON SERIES

A CORRESPONDENCE

Janet Malcolm and Marta Werner

When I first opened Marta Werner's *Emily Dickinson's Open Folios* I felt a shiver of interest and desire such as one feels in an expensive shop at the sight of an object of particular beauty and rarity. I was drawn to the book's right-hand pages on which typewritten words appeared – words that were wild and strange, and typing that evoked the world of the early-twentieth-century avant-garde. These were Marta Werner's transcriptions of scraps of handwritten prose by Emily Dickinson, discovered after her death. The scraps themselves were reproduced in facsimile opposite the typed transcripts.

The book belonged to my friend Sharon Cameron, a professor and critic and the author of two books on Emily Dickinson that are considered classics in the field. I was at her apartment. She had shown me the book – I forget for what reason – and I asked if I could cut out some of the right-hand pages to put into collages. She looked at me in horror and said, 'Certainly not.'

I tried to buy the book on Amazon and found it was out of print, and couldn't find it anywhere else. Sharon Cameron suggested I write to Marta Werner:

18 September 2012

Dear Marta Werner,

I have been trying to purchase a copy of your wonderful book *Emily Dickinson's Open Folios*, and have had no success. My friend Sharon Cameron suggested I write to you on the off chance that you had an extra copy I could buy from you, or that you could direct me to a source.

With thanks and best wishes,
Janet Malcolm

~

Dear Janet Malcolm,

How extremely kind of you to write!

It's rather strange, I suppose, but I have only one copy of the book. I believe my mother has one, too, though, so since there's one floating about the family somewhere, I'd be happy to send you my copy. I certainly don't want anything for it.

If you'd accept my copy, I'd be delighted to send it. It seems to belong to another part of my life – I hope I learned from it!

All my best,
Marta

~

19 September 2012

Dear Marta,

I cannot tell you how moved I am by your offer to give me your only copy of the book. Your generosity is staggering. Of course I accept with enormous pleasure and gratitude. May I, in inadequate return, send you a copy of my book *Burdock*, a collection of photographs of burdock leaves that grew in the New England countryside? If so, would you send me your mail address? My address is [. . .].

With huge thanks and all best wishes,
Janet

~

Dear Janet,

Thank you so much for accepting the book. It is a small thing, after all, and I fear you will definitely lose in this trade. Please don't regret it too deeply!

Of course I would be delighted to have *Burdock* – and it could not come at a better time. I am just starting work on the field notebooks of a rather obscure early-twentieth-century naturalist – Cordelia Stanwood – and your photographs – and especially your essay – will press me forward through uncertain beginnings. My address is [. . .].

It seems somehow rude, or cliché, or some combination of both, to tell you how much I admire your work. But it is true, so I'll say it anyway, and hope I don't embarrass you.

Gratefully,
Marta

~

Dear Marta,

I'm so glad that you know my work and like it. If there is any other book (or books) of mine I could send along with *Burdock*, would you let me know?

All my best,
Janet

~

20 September 2012

Dear Janet,

How generous! But I think I have everything!
    Open Folios is winging its way to you.

Thank you for taking it . . .
Marta

~

25 September 2012

Dear Janet,

Burdock is here. It is beautiful.
    It came at a strange time. My mother is very ill, and when I look
at the leaves – pristine and ravaged at once – I think of her.
    She would love them, too, without making the comparison.
    Thank you so much.

All my best,
Marta

~

26 September 2012

Dear Marta,

Your remarkable book has arrived, with your lovely inscription, and,
again, I am so very grateful and cannot thank you enough. I am

curious about the transcriptions. They look as if they were done on various old typewriters. Did you do them? I am very sorry to hear about your mother's illness. How hard this must be for you. I send all my best wishes for her recovery.

Janet

~

27 September 2012

Dear Janet,

I'm so glad the book arrived. The transcriptions are indeed my own – and what a trial! I was working on the book so many years ago – in the early 1990s – and so the possibilities (technologically speaking) were rather limited. And, beyond this problem, far beyond it, was my great uncertainty about what an 'ideal' transcript of a Dickinson poem would look like. In the end, I decided I wanted to do a few seemingly contradictory things: call attention to the 'alienness' of the transcript – its distance, temporal and iconic, etc. – from the manuscript; show and partly enact the conflict between the regularity of type (or typesetting) and the singularity of the hand; and break down distinctions between prose and verse by insisting on following Dickinson's physical line breaks. I'm not at all sure these intentions – such as they were – translate to readers, but this was what was in my mind. And I think the spirit of Melville was working in all this too – and a story I heard about Melville insisting on always adding the punctuation to those of his works transcribed by others – his sister & wife. In transcribing Dickinson, the excessiveness of certain letters and marks fought and won over the regularizing typewriter.

And yes, initially I did do the transcriptions on typewriters. My grandfather had an amazing (if worthless!) collection of typewriters, which I commandeered for the occasion. Now I am quite sure I would proceed differently! But honestly, I still do not know exactly how. [. . .]

Thank you very much for the good thoughts about my mother. When I see her in a few weeks, I will bring *Burdock* to show her. I am sure she will be moved.

At the end of the book, you mention a particular way in which the original photographs were transformed. Do these photographs in the book look so very different from your originals?

I am sure you have seen Dickinson's herbarium?

I have a question about an exquisite sentence in your introduction – something about the ongoing project of decontextualization. But I will have to ask it later, since I don't have the sentence before me. When I read it, it struck me as related to the whole problem (or interest!) of the transcript, and I wanted to pursue it further.

About a year before my father died, we took up the habit – he started it – of sending each other lists of the numbers of Dickinson poems we liked. We did not comment at all on the selections – simply exchanged them every few weeks over the course of several months. The experience was slightly uncanny, and it struck me last night that one could do such a thing with the burdock leaves. That is, that they might be exchanged as messages. The more I look at them, the more they seem to say – or at least the more I talk to myself.

Thank you so much.
Marta

~

29 September 2012

Dear Marta,

Many things in your letter – especially the mention of decontextualization – tell me that the time has come to tell you of the special reason why I wanted a copy of your book – namely, to cut some pages out of it and put them into collages. When I saw the book at Sharon Cameron's house, this desire formed itself in my mind – I began to 'see' the collages. It was the typewritten transcriptions rather than the handwritten originals that stirred my imagination. The series I want to make will also use images and charts from astronomical texts. Before starting the 'cutting' and 'scissoring' (the words leaped out of your text) of your precious only copy, I want to have your permission to do so. I will completely understand if you would prefer I not do so, and will continue my search for another copy.

The way the burdock photographs are printed makes them softer-edged and more painterly. The prints themselves are much better than the reproductions in the book. If you ever come to New York, I would be happy to show the prints to you. Some are at the Lori Bookstein Fine Art and the Davis & Langdale galleries and others are under my bed.

Your use of the word uncanny resonates with me. Doesn't it apply to our encounter?

All my best,
Janet

~

Dear Janet,

Oh but of course – cut away! I can think of no better fate for the pages of this last copy of my first book than to become collages made by your hands. And to have as company astronomical texts and charts – that is perfectly lovely. There is one – I think it's A 742 – which is very torn and cut, I wonder if you will be drawn to it . . . And another – I think A 757? – where one word, 'Last', is written upside down and under other text. The word 'Last' is written in a beautiful, magnified fair-copy hand, the text that covers it is in the small, contracted hand of the working drafts. I wonder so much which ones will summon you. I only wish I had the original typescripts to send you. I moved several times since making them and, each time, things vanished, as they do. I shall search again, and if I find them, I will send them on to you – if only as curiosities.

I would love to see the burdock prints, in the galleries and under the bed, though I would not want to put you to any trouble!

As for uncanny encounters – yes – this meeting between us is as you say. And I value it all the more for the attending strangeness. There is not enough of this in correspondences – or friendships.

Gratefully,
Marta

~

30 September 2012

Dear Marta,

I am so happy that my project has your blessing, and will start work on it today. I will let you know which fragments I 'appropriate' as it's called. The book is in my studio and I am about to go out and buy fresh glue.

With many, many thanks again,
Janet

THE EMILY DICKINSON SERIES

Janet Malcolm

Courtesy of the artist and
Lori Bookstein Fine Art, New York
Photos by Etienne Frossard

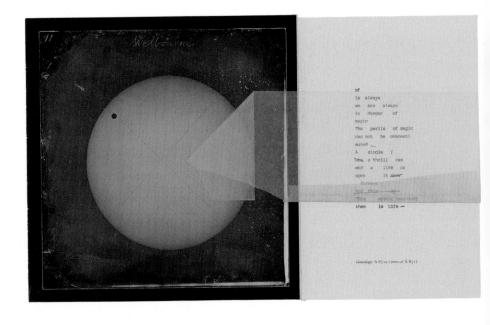

of
is always
we are always
in danger of
magic
The perils of magic
can not be oversti
mated —
A single /
Ume, a thrill can
end a life or
open it anew
forever
And this —
This mystic territory
then is Life —

Genealogy: A 871a (verso of A 871)

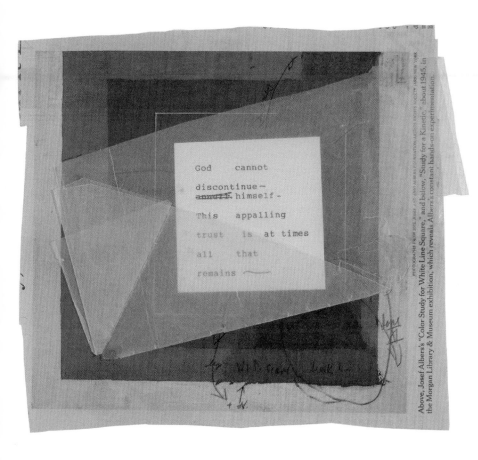

God   cannot

discontinue —
~~annul it~~ himself -

This   appalling

trust   is at times

all   that

remains —

Above, Josef Albers's "Color Study for White Line Square," and below, "Study for a Kinetic," about 1945, in the Morgan Library & Museum exhibition, which reveals Albers's constant hands-on experimentation.

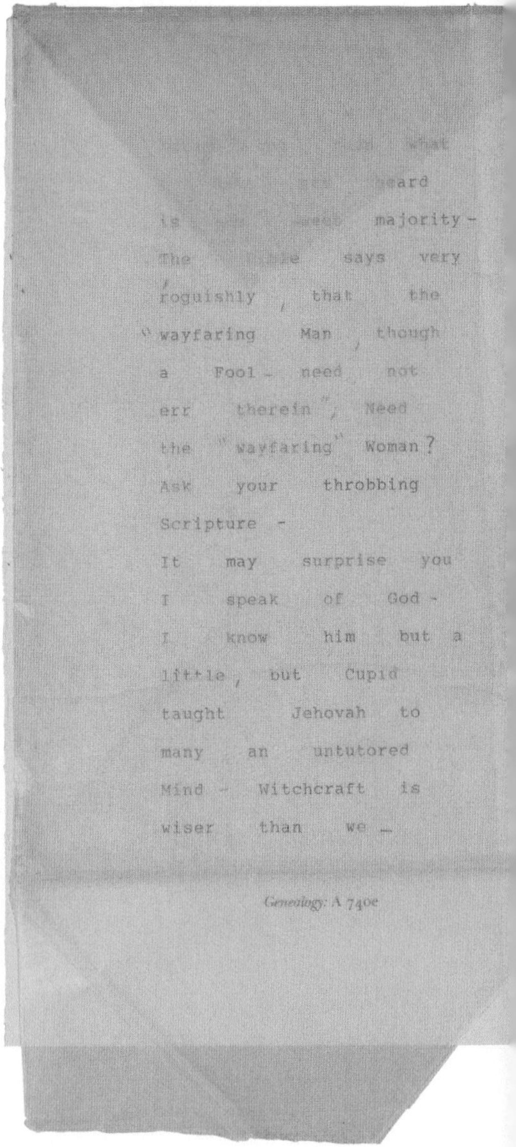

... what
... heard
is ... majority –
The ... says very
roguishly, that the
"wayfaring Man, though
a Fool, need not
err therein", Need
the "wayfaring" Woman?
Ask your throbbing
Scripture –
It may surprise you
I speak of God –
I know him but a
little, but Cupid
taught Jehovah to
many an untutored
Mind – Witchcraft is
wiser than we –

Genealogy: A 740e

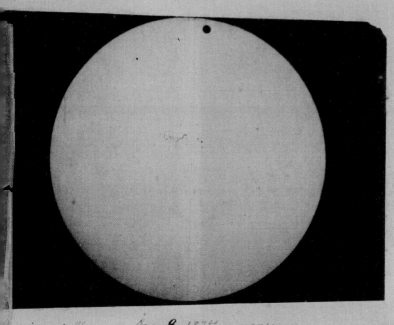

ansit of Venus - Dec. 9, 1874. 1874.

To Mr. Alfred B. Riggs

From his friend

Chas. W. Raymond
Capt. of Engineers. U.S. Army
Chief Astronomer.

4. *Vinnie*

<del>terested</del> _ thanks
very much
<del>was very</del>
<del>teresting</del> How it
ould interest mo
her / each of
s exclaimed —
know / you will
emember her with
ever ceasing love —
he never seemed
lderly to us
nd we think
f her in a
weet prime we
an scarcely
xpress —
innie gives her
ove —
others Brother
Good night

home she is
rested and pleased
Thank you for
loving her and
please to tell my
Cousins how beau
tiful she was —
We hope you are
having a lovely
Winter and think
of with new
peace in the
warmth of your
Home
Daughters — Accept
our love for them
and a kiss for
the little Grand
Boy — Vinnie
received the
paper — and
<del>was much</del>

Genealogy: A 748a *(verso)* [early 1883? (Johnson)]

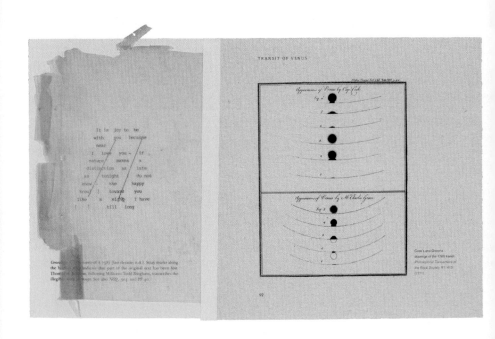

It is joy to be
with you because
near
I love you ~ if
nature means a
distinction at late
as tonight do not
know the happy
from I toward you
like a sight I have
till long

Greetings from the coast of A 756 [too elevate; n.d.]. Strap marks along the bottom edge indicate that part of the original text has been lost. Thoreau et Jackson, following Millicent Todd Bingham, transcribes the illegible text as such. See also NJ55, 515 and PF 911.

Cook's and Green's
drawings of the 1769 transit.
Philosophical Transactions of
the Royal Society, 61, 410
(1771).

92

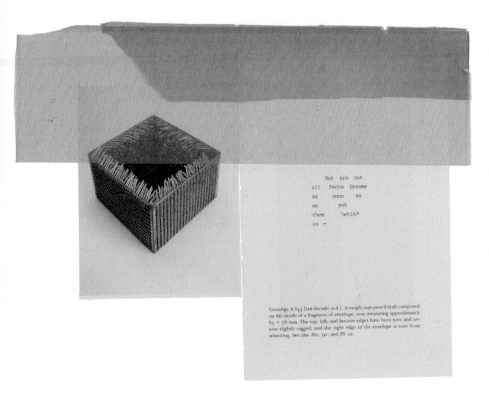

But are not
all   Facts   Dreams
as   soon   as
we   put
them   behind
us —

Genealogy: A 843 [last decade; n.d.]. A rough copy pencil draft composed
on the inside of a fragment of envelope, now measuring approximately
85 × 78 mm. The top, left, and bottom edges have been torn and are
now slightly ragged, and the right edge of the envelope is wavy from
scissoring. See also *Rev.,* 91; and PF 22.

6. *Facts*

7. *Improbable*

```
I    wonder    we

ever    leave    the

Improbable ~ it  is

so  fair   a  Home,

and  ,perhaps  we

dont –

What    is    half

so    improbable
```

Genealogy: A 746 [about 1880; 1882?]. A fragment of a fair copy pencil draft composed on a partial sheet (top half torn away) of wove, off-white stationery, possibly watermarked IRISH LINEN FABRIC and now measuring approximately 89 × 123 mm. The top and left edges of the document have been carefully torn along a straight line. See also *Rei.*, 87; and *L* 645.

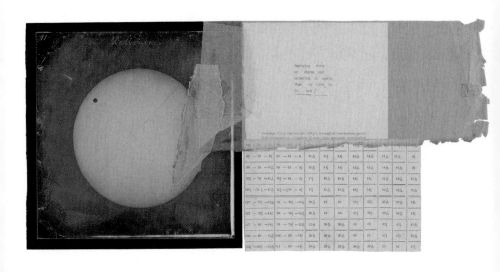

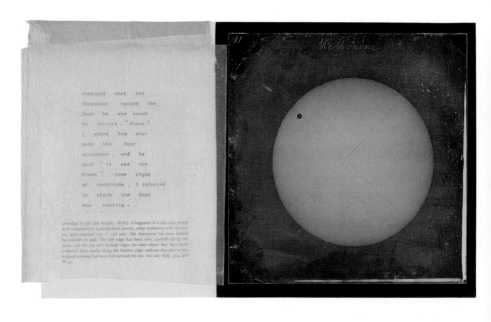

remained what the
Carpenter called the
Door he was asked
to correct. "Plumb",
I asked him what
made the Door
erroneous, and he
said "it was not
Plumb". Some rigor
of rectitude, I inferred
in which the Door
was wanting —

Genealogy & 758 (list decade; 1858). A fragment of a fair copy (good draft composed on a partial sheet of wove, white stationery, now measuring approximately 125 × 158 mm. The document has been folded horizontally in half. The left edge has been carefully along the spine, and the top and bottom edges are wavy where they have been scissored. Iron marks along the bottom edge indicate that part of the original message has been lost beyond the tear. See also MQ, 505, and W 45.

10. *Melbourne*

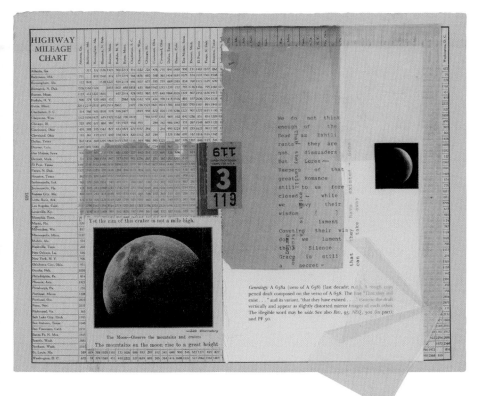

11. *Crater*

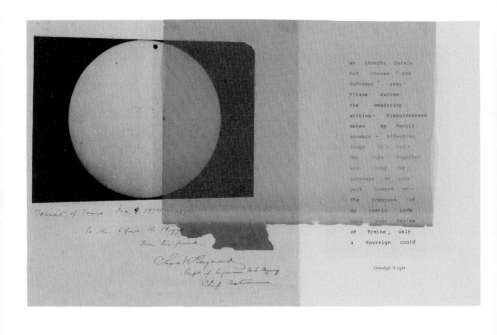

12. *Ermine*

AMERICAN VOGUE

Edmund White

Edmund White (right), with Michel Foucault, 1983
© Patrick O'Connor

O f course, I'd lied to the editors of *Vogue* and told them I spoke perfect French.

My first assignment was to interview Eric Rohmer, the most intellectual of all French film directors, an elderly genius obsessed by *midinettes* ('shopgirls'). And yet in 1984 he was only sixty-four, which naturally seemed ancient to me then. Someone had said that seeing his movies was 'kind of like watching paint dry'. I preferred what my friend Jacques Fieschi had said, that Rohmer was 'this sensual intellectual'.

Rohmer had been born Maurice Henri Joseph Schérer. I'd admired his talky films *Claire's Knee* and *Ma Nuit chez Maude*. I'd rehearsed my questions carefully with Gilles Barbedette, who'd translated my novel *Nocturnes for the King of Naples*. I had to tape Rohmer's answers since I had no idea what he was saying – which of course meant that I couldn't pose any follow-up questions to the provocative and original things he said. In Hollywood movies the star absorbs and perfects the foreign language seamlessly, and in a matter of days, since language plays no part in the plot. But my fear of daunting linguistic encounters only added to my mounting agoraphobia: I seldom left the apartment. I'd sit in a chair and rehearse what I might say, what Rohmer might say and how I'd answer, and hours of invented conversations would play out in my head. I'd think something in English and immediately try to translate it into French. I'd practise translation so much that I could say many things, at least the sort of things that typically I'd say in my own language. Comprehension, however, was another thing altogether. After I'd presented my own carefully displayed sentence like a diamond necklace on black velvet, the other speaker, the French person, would throw his sentence at me like a handful of wet sand. It would sting so badly that I'd wince, and an instant later I would wonder what had just happened to me. Perhaps worst of all, I failed to grasp little nice things shopkeepers or neighbours were saying about the weather or the wild strawberries, pleasant comments I was unable to acknowledge and engage with. John Purcell, my American boyfriend who'd come over with me from New York, couldn't speak but could understand, and together we made up an inept sort of team. What I could do was read French books and look up the words. Sometimes now when I glance over the novels and non-fiction works I was patiently annotating in those days, it astonishes me that there was ever a time when I didn't know those words.

I'd lie on the couch and read and read. Marie-Claude, a literary scout and my best friend in Paris, who knew the publicity girls at all the publishing houses, had put me on every list for freebies; in addition she'd call to nudge them along if she was excited about a particular title. She'd say, 'But Monsieur White *is* American *Vogue* in Paris,' letting them imagine I might write up an obscure first novel and start a bidding war for it in the States.

What I learned soon enough was that American magazine editors weren't interested in anything happening in France unless it was happening to other Americans: a hit play where the audience had to vote every night whether to behead Marie Antoinette or not? No interest. The reopening after many years of the Musée Guimet, one of the great collections of Asian art? No interest. Fashion was interesting since anyone could buy it and everyone would eventually be affected by it. A lawsuit by Margaret Mitchell's heirs against Régine Desforges, a Frenchwoman who'd adapted the plot of *Gone with the Wind* to France during World War II (the Nazis were the Yankees) was interesting since it dealt with an American classic and an American legal victory (though eventually Desforges beat the plagiarism rap and her book became a successful television film in 2000).

Fortunately I didn't understand the limitations of my role as an American cultural reporter in France until I'd read hundreds of books and looked up thousands of words – many of them time and again. At one point it occurred to me that I had to look up the same word five times before I'd learned it. And of course I nearly always got the gender wrong. Jane Birkin, an English actress who sang in French in a high, squeaky voice, in interviews always confused the *le* and the *la* and French comedians impersonating her always used this habit of hers as the basis of their send-ups. I remember once saying '*la mariage*' and a five-year-old corrected me: 'But it's *le mariage*.' Quickly, her mother, blushing, whispered to the little girl, 'Don't correct Monsieur. He's a professor.'

In the winters it was grey and would rain every day, but my apartment was snug and had good heat. I lay on my couch, actually a daybed, and read. I had just two rooms – a bedroom twice the size of the double bed with tall French windows looking out on the slanting roof of the St-Louis-en-l'Île Church with its upended stone volute like a colossal snail that had broken through the rain-slicked tiles and was inching down toward the gutters at geological speed. The sitting room was larger, with two windows, a desk, a basket chair, a dining-room table and the daybed in an alcove. The apartment had been the study of the landlady's deceased husband, an epigraphist, and on the walls held up by metal brackets were ancient stones inscribed by the Romans, marble fragments he'd excavated in Algeria.

Language problems guided me in my choice of friends. Women, especially old bourgeois women, spoke more clearly than their male or their younger counterparts. The very speech patterns (emphatic, precise) I might have found annoying in English came to me in French as a blessing. My favourite old woman was my landlady, Madame Pflaum, an Austrian who'd lived in Paris since the 1930s. She had me to tea with her best friend. The two women had known each other for over forty years but still addressed each other as *vous* and used 'Madame Pflaum' and 'Madame Dupont'. Perhaps because she was a foreigner, Madame Pflaum spoke her adopted language with unusual care.

At the gym I met Barbara, a girl with a pretty, chubby face and an almost neurotic level of curiosity, and I cherished her for her clear enunciation, her avoidance of slang and her linguistic patience. Like any good teacher, Barbara took my cloudy, twisted sentences and reworked them into model phrases out of a textbook.

Barbara had divorced parents – an architect father who worked in his spacious studio overlooking a garden and a batty, out-of-work mother who lived in a project for the poor, an 'HLM' (*Habitation de Loyer Moyen*, or medium-rent housing), located in a sleek skyscraper that Pompidou had thrown up in La Défense in the 1970s to modernize the capital, rival New York and ultimately destroy the Parisian skyline. Fortunately for Parisians, Pompidou would die before he could commit more mischief.

Barbara had sex on the brain and always wanted to know what different boys in the gym looked like naked in the locker room. She either was slightly dim or pretended to be. Over and over she'd ask me her slow, precise, primary questions about homosexuality.

'Now tell me, Edmond, have you ever tried sex with a woman? Are you afraid of the vagina? Do you think that there are teeth in there?'

But no matter how irritating her questions might be, she spoke clearly and slowly and always corrected my French in an inoffensive and automatic way. For instance, I had a habit of interchangeably using the adjectives *immense*, *grand* and *gros*, yet Barbara had assigned a different nuance to each word. She was also a stickler for the progression of tenses – only a pluperfect could be nested inside a past clause. Despite her careful and kind ministrations, I never mastered these nuances. Barbara suggested I buy *Le Grevisse*, a thousand-page grammar text with which every French person is familiar. That this pedantry coexisted with an unhealthy or obsessive sexual curiosity should not have surprised me. What is certain is that if she were a mumbler, as many of us Americans are, I'd never have had anything to do with her. I envied her because she dated a slender young Czech,

Pavel, with a mild, gentle manner and a large, uncircumcised penis, which he would towel-dry at length while chatting affably with me in the locker room. Then again, there was always a bit of seduction in the air.

At the gym I only met ordinary French office workers who like people everywhere led a treadmill existence called, colloquially, '*Métro-Boulot-Dodo*' – Parisian slang for 'Subway-Work-Bed'.

At Marie-Claude's dinners no one spoke in any predictable way. They were all intellectuals and writers who I learned had to show how ironic they could be, how droll, how quickly and easily they could anticipate every objection their interlocutors might make. The advancement of a simple idea or piece of information was not the object. The task was to show they were civilized beings who caught every allusion. They were capable of enclosing linguistic brackets inside conversational parentheses.

Moreover, they interrupted constantly which, it amazed me to learn, was not considered rude in Paris. Madame de Staël in her book about Germany had written that German was not a proper language for intelligent conversation since you had to wait till the end of the sentence to hear the verb and couldn't interrupt. I found interruptions especially irritating because I needed my full allotments of airtime in order to stagger toward my point.

But France, more than any other culture, is a tight, silver skein of names and references and half-stated allusions. Whereas America is so populous that even the writers don't know all the names of the other writers, in France the members of the general educated public recognize the names of all French writers, whether they've read them or not. Of course it helps that writers are so often interviewed on television and by the press. What is true of writers is true of every other category of civilized experience; everyone knows the name and address of the best pastry-maker, the best source of bed linens and napery, the best caterer, the best saddle- and harness-maker. They're listed in every middle-class person's mental collection of *les bonnes adresses*. Porthault for sheets. Hédiard for food. Berthillon for sherbets and ice creams, so confident of its status that it closed for the entire month of August. Failure to know any one of these names can even suggest inferior social origins.

This little world is a ball that is always in the air, bounced from hand to hand. Maybe it aids the native speakers that French (not Spanish, as everyone says) is spoken more rapidly than any other tongue, facilitating an unequalled density of reference and qualification. The composer Virgil Thomson, who lived a third of his long life in France, once pointed out that the French never grope for a word or stutter or go blank and say, 'Uh . . .' He suggested that the French, unlike us, have what today we'd call a social GPS, an instant device for orienting themselves and navigating their way through their own culture, whereas we are not only often at a loss for words but also for opinions. The maddening confidence of the French (about the sequence three cheeses should be eaten in, from mildest to strongest, about exactly when to arrive at a party and when to leave, about how to sign off in a friendly but correct formal letter) fills in all social, and verbal, blanks.

I quickly learned that for a linguistic neophyte like me, the most difficult encounter to deal with was a party attended by a group of friends who'd all known one another forever. They'd be hard enough to cope with if they were speaking English since even then they'd all be talking in shorthand. In French, they became incomprehensible.

The easiest social situation, I found, was talking to one person who was in love with you, someone who was studying your face for the slightest frown of confusion. The eyes, I figured out, always betray a failure to understand. If I didn't want to flag my distress at a small dinner party or provoke a tedious explanation made merely for my benefit, I lowered my eyes like a Japanese bride. A *diner à deux* is the easiest exchange because we quickly become accustomed to a lover's accent, turn of mind, range of reference and vocabulary – and he or she instantly gears his or her words to our level of comprehension.

After a party the most difficult event is a narrative French film, in which the actors usually speak more carelessly than random individuals do on the street. Mumbling is proof of artistic verisimilitude. A television newscast is the next most difficult occasion since it usually depends on a vocabulary and metaphors peculiar to itself. As a foreigner I realized what a closed world the news is for all but the initiated, an obscurity that is obviously worrying in a democracy.

Some American or French friends who were bilingual wondered why I was spending so much time with kids from the gym. I was too embarrassed to admit that I had chosen these particular kids for the slow, clear way they spoke French. When the great writer Emmanuel Carrère and his wife came to dinner, they teased me for my 'adolescent evenings' (*tes soirées ado*).

Marie-Claude would not countenance my complaints about agonizing over French.

'But your French is perfect!' she said in English.

She and I spoke English all the time except at her dinner parties, where she'd invite the latest literary star to bask in our short-lived adoration. I'd been put through similar paces when *A Boy's Own Story* had come out in France (*Un Jeune Américain*). I'd assumed that a charming older gay man, the editor of *Science et Vie*, was actually interested in me personally and would want to see me often in the future. In fact, I'd made a modest little splash and the editor as a true Parisian needed to know everyone and everything *dans le vent, à la page, au courant* – all ways of referring to what's new, the latest manifestation of *l'air du temps*.

Of course journalists back in New York had to keep up with the latest trends but wouldn't have invited the trend over to dinner. New Yorkers were always exhausted after their twelve hours at the office and two hours at the gym and an hour at the shrink's; when they got home, they would crawl into a hot bath, and from there to a huge immaculate bed where they ate their plate of lobster ravioli and watched a talk show until they sank into restless, clamorous sleep. They couldn't be bothered to see their oldest friends, much less a total stranger. A friend in New York in fact was defined as someone you never needed to see, who would never get angry at you for ignoring him.

In Paris, however, there were still rituals in place for promising new people, new ideas, new trends (which a bit later, in the nineties, would eventually be colloquially labelled *tendance*, or 'tendency'). Something new was said to be '*très tendance*'. If you were a mere trend, no one wanted to be stuck with seeing you more than once; the host expected you to stay on message during your single visit and communicate clearly what was new about you and your work.

I'd written a novel about my life as a tormented teen in the Midwest in the 1950s. It was hailed in the English-speaking world because it was seen as well written, at once a breakthrough thematically and an 'instant classic'. The French, however, couldn't quite grasp the novelty or the importance of my accomplishment. After all France was the country of Proust, André Gide and Jean Genet – three of the most celebrated innovators of the twentieth century who all wrote quite openly about being gay: Gide's journals and his memoir, *If It Die*, as well as his early novel *The Immoralist*; Genet's *Our Lady of the Flowers* and his four other novels; Proust's entire oeuvre, in which so many of the men and women turn out to be homosexual (though the narrator doesn't). How could my slender volume compare to these massive achievements, which had preceded it by fifty, seventy, eighty years?

Nor did the French like the whole idea of 'gay fiction', though they'd invented it. France was opposed to the notion of identity politics and even more so to the literature of special interest groups. In France there was no black novel, no Jewish novel, certainly no gay novel. To be sure, Jews wrote about being Jewish but everyone, Jewish and Gentile alike, regarded with horror the category of 'the Jewish novel' (though there had been a brief flurry of Jewish fiction at the beginning of the last century after the Dreyfus Affair).

If specific identities were rejected in France, it was in favour of 'universalism', a concept so dear to the Enlightenment and the Revolution, the ideal of the abstract citizen, stripped of all qualifications, equal to everyone else before the voting urn and the court of justice. In the arts it meant that the individual with all his quirks was thrown into high relief but the group he belonged to was pushed into the background. French schoolchildren in history class did not learn about Napoleon's 'Corsican' heritage, just as in literature class no one mentioned that Proust's mother was Jewish (nor had Proust himself mentioned it). Proust made his narrator heterosexual and his family Catholic so that against this gold standard of propriety he could describe in detail his lesbians, his intergenerational gays, his gay sadists and rent boys and more broadly the secret world of homosexuality that infuses the visible world of class and age distinctions. His contemporaries congratulated Proust on his 'courage' in exploring the twisted world of homosexuality, since he said nothing to enlighten them about his own orientation. The only trouble with universalism was that if it had been progressive originally, now it had become conservative.

Translation is always difficult. The lush metaphors of my *Nocturnes for the King of Naples*, so slippery in English, had to be sorted out in French. Time and again, of a figurative conceit I'd carefully crafted, I was told, 'But you can't mean both things in French.' Even the word 'boy' (*garçon*) was suspect; it sounded too much like a waiter or a paedophile's delight. That's why *A Boy's Own Story* was translated as *Un Jeune Américain*. I wanted it to be called *Signes de piste* (a 1930s collection of Boy Scout novels) or even *Feu de camp*, but I don't think any French person understood what I was getting at.

Not that the French were impervious to the allure of the exotic, but they preferred to locate the Other beyond the elsewhere. Within France they wanted everything to be uniform, starting with themselves. No wonder those French living in the capital resented the question, 'Where are you from?'

'Paris, why do you ask? I've lived in Paris all my life.'

'And before that?'

'Marseille. Surely you can't hear the accent?'

'Not a trace.'

'But is there anything I do differently from all other Parisians?'

'Of course not. You wear the same dark clothes and are just

as skinny and murmur just as softly and take the same group tours to the same places like Vietnam and Anatolia or Pharaonic Egypt and have never toured France itself. You know the canals of Venice better than your own medieval monastery of Moissac or the chalets of Franche-Comté – though your grandparents still vacation close to home.'

Reassured, your friend smiles and says, 'I still don't understand.'

'In America, we're proud of our regional and national differences. We say, "What are you?" and the answer is "Irish" or "Italian", though our ancestors came over from Galway in the 1840s. "Where are you from?" people ask. The answer might be "Arkansas, my mother never wore shoes till she was ten", and we're proud of this.'

Your interlocutor will then say, 'In France we have no class differences in our way of speaking and only four slight, very slight, regional accents, impossible for a foreigner to detect.'

'The Provençal accent is easy enough, like when they say "vang" for vin, or "pang" for pain.'

'But no one says "pang"!'

I can remember when Hector Bianciotti, an Argentine novelist living in Paris, interviewed me for a two-page piece in the *Nouvel Observateur*, a weekly left-of-centre glossy, roughly equivalent to the weekend magazine of the English *Guardian*. He and I met in the downstairs bar at the Montalembert a few doors from the offices of Gallimard, the premier publisher. The room with its brown velvet walls and heavy leather club chairs had been a meeting place for writers since the time of Sartre and Beauvoir, who'd more famously also liked the Café de Flore three blocks away. I had seen photos of Sartre taken here with his followers including his handsome secretary Jean Cau. In another photo Jean Genet was being introduced to the author of *La Bâtarde*, Violette Leduc. She was upset that day because Genet said, 'I've been enjoying your *Asphyxia*,' though the book was named *L'Asphixie* and not just *Asphyxie*. Genet's way of saying the title suggested that he was enjoying the feeling of moral and mental disarray in the work – or so she imagined in her hysterical, paranoid way. Like Genet, she was a fatherless child, as was their wealthy patron, Jacques Guérin – another 'bastard'. (Ironically, later the three bastards would collaborate on a short black-and-white film about a baptism in which Genet played the baby.)

Hector asked me a few random questions about my *enfance dans le Ohio*, and rather than tossing off a witty remark or two, I started giving a complete report: '. . . then, at age seven, I moved from Cincinnati to Evanston, Illinois.' At last I noticed the look of panic and even disdain crossing Hector's face. 'I don't need to know all that. It's just an article, not a hagiography!'

When the article appeared in print, it had several mistakes in it and my friend Gilles said, 'It's of no importance. No one will remember. No one will even finish reading it.'

I mentioned that in America we had fact-checkers and that we had to put red pencil dots over every statement after we'd verified it from three sources. Gilles merely waved a hand as if driving away an annoying insect. When I went on pointing out the mistakes, Gilles said, 'My poor Ad.' He pronounced my name in what he believed was the authentic American way, Ad. 'I think you have no idea how important Hector is. He will probably win the Goncourt this year and soon he'll be a member of the French Academy. He's done you a tremendous honour.'

Hector had begun to write in French, not Spanish, only a few years previously. People said he was helped by his lover Angelo Rinaldi, a Corsican novelist and the extremely acerbic critic for *L'Express*. (Hector wrote one terrific book about his coming out in the Pampas, *Le Pas si lent de l'amour*.) In the years to come, Angelo would like every other book I wrote and hate the alternate ones. His vitriol in general won him lots of attention since most French critics were routinely positive. An older writer explained to me that during the Vichy years, right-wing critics had been so brutally nasty that ever since the left-wing style had been pleasantly anodyne; the slightest reservation was read as a violent dismissal. Gilles had been right about Hector, who was invited to join the Academy, and a few years later so was Angelo. I would often see Angelo, always grimacing, each time his hair a colour never encountered in nature, heading for his *chambre d'assignation* on the Île Saint-Louis, usually in the company of a teenager he'd met at a gym during wrestling practice.

I can't remember how, but in some way Milan Kundera became aware of me. He wanted someone to translate two of his political essays from French (which he'd recently begun writing in, too) into English. I told him I could not even translate a French menu in restaurants – was *confit de canard* 'duck preserved in its own fat'? And did a *financier* have something to do with cake or a pastry? Kundera said he didn't want anyone too sophisticated. '*Sophistiqué*' had kept in French some of its original sense of sophistry, of an ingenious playing with words, and I took it that what Kundera hated was what Fowler in his *Modern English Usage* calls 'elegant variation' – the pointless and confusing interchanging of near-synonyms so that the reader thinks something new is being discussed.

At the time Kundera was very fearful that the Czech equivalent of the KGB was trying to bump him off so I had to buzz him precisely at noon, neither a minute before nor a minute later, and I'd be accompanied by his wife Vera up to the first landing of his rue Littré apartment. Then he would walk with me up the last flight of stairs. If he was famous as a wrestler, he must have been a featherweight because he was very frail, though his pictures made him look big and powerful. He didn't know English very well. He knew that *about* meant 'more or less' but he didn't know it was also a preposition, as in 'about love'. We wrangled over many words in that way. His essays, as I recall, were about the spurious idea that Prague was closer culturally to Paris than Petersburg. His own father had been a musician for Janáček in Brno and I wanted to point out that Janáček had adapted a Russian play (Ostrovsky's *The Storm*) in *Kát'a Kabanová* and not a French one, but I didn't dare. Yet he was very sweet and played a record for me of one of Janáček's chamber works and gave me a running commentary on its secret plot: 'Here he sees her again about to board the train.' His wife fed me a treasured

Czech recipe which was so garlicky that the next day Marie-Claude wordlessly gave me chlorophyll gum and at the movies the couple in the row in front of us got up and took different seats when she and I sat down behind them.

My early, brief moment of Parisian celebrity came and went. Afterwards few people in France could place me but some gave troubled little smiles of recognition when my name was mentioned. '*Mais bien sûr*,' they whispered politely. This French system of making a fuss over whatever was new and then promptly forgetting it meant that many young innovators had their moment in the sun right away, without having to wait years as they would have to in America. But it also meant that new ideas – feminism, say, or gay liberation – weren't revolutionary or very interesting, since they were treated as this year's fad, no more, and quickly were cycled out of sight. In America an idea was accepted only after it was judged to be of real, lasting significance. Then it stuck around forever, especially if it became a department in American universities – gender studies or queer studies. If I'd introduce an American intellectual to French friends in the mid-1980s, and say, 'She's a leading feminist who's queering the Renaissance,' they'd make a face and say, 'Feminism. You mean that's still being discussed in America? We had that here in the early seventies, but it's hopelessly *vétuste, démodé*. No one ever mentions it. No more than any woman now would wear Berber jewellery or a tuxedo or a hoop skirt.' ∎

Toboggan Run

Midnight, early February. Moonlight, trapped
between the snow still falling and the white earth,
is luminous from our sloped roof to the firs
that edge the common land. In the white curve

of the field beyond, figures almost drowned
in the static interference of snow and distance
toboggan down the spills. They're so far off,
so dimly seen – a black speck riding the cataracts

and screes of our deepest snowfall in years.
Their runners leave the snow-warp as they leap,
like animals possessed beyond their strength –
spawning salmon, startled deer. What would I give

to be one of those swimmers in all this snow,
swallowed by the cold and the night's strange radiance?
Would I leave this house, its synthesis of brightness,
would I give myself to the wind? The snow pulls a veil

across the moonlit world, deepens and draws in
on figures lost to the year's last blizzard,
tobogganing a swerving run through our rarest weather,
on and on, liturgy or evensong or requiem for snow.

MY AVANT-GARDE EDUCATION

Bernard Cooper

ROBERT RAUSCHENBERG
Bed, 1955
© Estate of Robert Rauschenberg
DACS, London/VAGA, New York 2013

A few weeks before the freshman semester at the School of Visual Arts in New York, I found a bachelor apartment (I loved the suave and manly sound of it) on East 12th Street between 2nd and 3rd Avenue. The basement windows were level with the sidewalk, the legs of pedestrians blurring past. If I pulled down the shades, harried shadows raced across them till daylight faded. Late at night, the homeless migrated up 12th Street from the Bowery and rummaged through the building's trash cans; my dreams echoed with a tinny clatter and I often awoke from a shallow sleep with the desperate sense I'd been searching for something.

I purchased a single bed (testament to my sexual pessimism), and a wobbly bookshelf from Junk 'n' Stuff, the used-furniture store around the corner. On its shelves I kept, among a few other books, *Pop Art Redefined*, *Pop Art and After* and *Pop!*. Unfurnished and white and lit by the fluorescent tubes above the kitchenette, the room bore enough of a resemblance to a gallery or loft to make me feel that I inhabited my future, or at least some affordable corner thereof.

Junk 'n' Stuff was owned by the young married couple who lived directly across the hall. Beginning my first night in the apartment, the sounds of their fights wafted though the bathroom air vent, a series of muffled but escalating accusations followed by a volley of fleshy thumps. Each time I ran across them in the hall, they were trussed up by a new set of slings, crutches, plaster casts, Ace bandages or eyepatches, their wounds and bruises in ever-changing colours and locations. Back then, spousal abuse was not the public issue it is today, and I was stunned not only by the extent of their injuries, but by their displays of what appeared to be genuine affection. Before donning their sunglasses, they exchanged loving glances through blackened eyes, one of them graciously holding open the lobby door while the other hobbled through it.

Within those first few weeks, no college-freshman mishap was too far-fetched or clichéd to befall me. Food in the refrigerator grew velvety with mould. I shrank half my clothes at the laundromat. I once buzzed into the building a man who claimed to work for the phone company. He shat on the floor of the lobby and left.

The city was stranger than I expected. Or rather, I felt like such a stranger there; it failed to meet my expectations. If there were opportunities to meet or have sex with other men, my sense of geographical dislocation, my attention to matters of daily survival and plain fear prevented me from noticing. However, men whom I'd quickly passed on the street during the day would reappear in my fantasies at night. Without even thinking, I'd hoard erotic provocations, physical details I could conjure at will: the landlord's imposing shoulders in a tank top, the arch of a window shopper's ass.

I suppose I half hoped to meet another gay student once school began. And yet I hadn't entirely given up on the idea that a female might come along whose compelling beauty or artistic daring could detain, or even derail, me from the inevitable. But on the first day of class – it had the baffling title of Art Praxis – what struck me most about my fellow students was the collective bashfulness that prevented us from talking, joking around or introducing ourselves to one another as we waited for the teacher, already fifteen minutes late. As a group we seemed not only green as artists, but too unformed and introverted as people to give off any clear signals regarding our sexuality. A wall clock ticked. The radiator wheezed. Beyond the tall windows, clouds gathered over the city, buildings in the distance hazy from rain. A glum spell had fallen over the room, and just as I braced myself for disappointment, the instructor appeared in the doorway, crushing a cigarette beneath his heel and hyperventilating from his climb up three flights of stairs. Or so I supposed.

Rather than books or a briefcase, he carried a small tape recorder that he placed on the table at the head of the class. He looked at us for what seemed like a long time. Beneath a head of scraggly hair that was limp from the rain, his features were almost farcically large, yet his face possessed, as homely faces sometimes can, a crude appeal. Once he'd caught his breath, I fully expected him to call roll, hand out a syllabus or engage in some academic formality that would let us know we were in the Big League now – no dabblers or dilettantes, please. Instead, he said, 'I ran all the way from SoHo while counting.' He punched a button on the tape recorder, left the classroom and paced in the hallway, occasionally peering through the open door to check our response to his 'piece'.

From the very start you could hear the impact of his feet on the pavement, faint blows pulsing in his breath. Soon he began to struggle for air, counting with a hollow rasp. By the time he reached two hundred, he'd succumbed to a rapid, dog-like pant. His tongue sounded dry. Sometimes he'd cough, muffling the numbers. It was difficult to listen to him without feeling exhausted or thirsty or starved for oxygen yourself. By then we were glancing at one another to make sure we weren't alone in our puzzlement or, in some cases, disgust. One student asked if it was too late to go to the registrar's office and get a refund, and a few kids snickered in solidarity. As he approached five hundred, you could barely make out which numbers he was heaving, the act of counting painfully abstract. Alternating waves of agitation and boredom beset the class. Nearly twenty minutes had passed. 'What does this have to do with art?' someone barked from the back of the room.

'That's good,' Mr Acconci shouted from the hallway. 'An excellent question. Thank you.' He lit a cigarette.

Finally the tape unspooled, its loose end slapping the opposite reel. Someone applauded, but it was unclear whether he did so out of appreciation or because the counting had finally stopped. Even in the silence, numbers continued to throb in my body, like the phantom sensation of rocking after you've been on a boat. Mr Acconci returned to the room with a weary expression (he had, after all, jogged twenty blocks). He turned off the tape recorder and glanced at his watch. 'That's all we have time for today.' Someone groaned with facetious disappointment, but Acconci impressed me as a man so thoroughly focused on his own peculiar ideas that he hardly noticed when they were met with derision. I found myself captivated by, and envious of, his self-possession. He cleared his throat. 'Your assignment for the next class . . .' Notebooks opened. Pens were poised. '. . . is to bring in nothing.'

'Hold it,' said Delia, the black girl who sat in front of me. 'Are you saying there's no assignment, or what?'

'I'm saying the assignment is to bring in nothing.'

'Zero?' asked Carl Tornquist, a boy with lank blond hair and wire-rimmed glasses.

'Is that how you interpret the assignment?'

Carl shrugged and bit the end of his pencil.

'Is it possible to make a work of art that is not embodied in an object?'

A ponderous silence.

'Well?' said Delia.

'Is it the artist's job to answer questions, or to ask them?'

In a classroom in Manhattan on a rainy day, my perception of art was changed forever. Vito Acconci's pedagogy was a mixture of persistent enquiry, faith in the invisible and nudges toward the unknown. It struck me for the first time that art might exist beyond the realms of painting and sculpture. This was a mind-boggling revelation, like opening a door in your own house and discovering an entirely new room. My jaw went lax, my breathing deepened. The spirit of conceptualism had entered me, and I became a convert then and there.

'Will we be graded on nothing?' asked Delia.

'Not,' said Acconci, 'if you come empty-handed.'

The next morning, while mulling over the nature of nothing, I sipped the instant coffee I'd made with hot tap water. I thought of the residue absences left: wet rings on the surface of a table, the rubbery crumbs when a word was erased. Nothingness took so many forms, each of them elusive. I considered handing in a blank sheet of paper, but that was too obvious a solution to the assignment, and I was sure another student had already thought of it. I racked my brain and pressed ahead. Wasn't it every artist's assignment to make something out of nothing for the rest of their lives? Wandering the paths of free association is the only skill I can boast I was born with, and so, sitting cross-legged on the floor of my apartment, I incubated odd ideas.

Eventually, I decided to write one of my secrets on a piece of paper. I'd use lemon juice instead of ink, a trick I'd learned from a Hardy Boys book in which the boys held an invisible message above a candle flame until the letters were cooked to a legible brown. As the elements of my project came together, a strange chill spread over my skin. For a blissful instant, chaos was shapely.

When I heard the couple across the hall making their early-morning manoeuvres into the outside world, I dashed out my door and asked if I could borrow a candle, a lemon and a pack of matches. They responded to my request without asking a single question, the kind of incurious etiquette they expected in return. While we made small talk, the husband blocked the door to their apartment, as if he were trying to prevent me from seeing inside. Finally the wife limped out holding a votive candle and matches in one hand and a wrinkled, anaemic lemon in the other. They nodded and donned dark glasses when I thanked them, walking arm in arm toward the door.

Back on the floor of my apartment, I squeezed lemon juice into a bowl. I needed a toothpick to use as a pen, and I found one spearing a shrivelled sandwich in the refrigerator. But when it came time to commit a secret to paper, I found myself baulking. My deepest secret was far too incriminating to share with a group of strangers, and yet the temptation to do so gave me a thrill, like curling my toes over the edge of a precipice and daring myself to look down. Though I'm not particularly proud of the fact that, in the end, I opted to maintain my secret by being oblique and thought of this as a practice run that would make my eventual honesty possible. *Sometimes I'm Afraid,*

I wrote. This statement managed to touch on the truth without actually jarring it loose.

Along with typewritten instructions – *Light candle. Hold paper six inches above flame. Burn secret after reading* – I neatly arranged everything in the clear plastic pouch my shaving kit had come in. Since Pop Art had made me too ardent a lover of objects to entirely forsake them, packaging an idea as if it were a product seemed like a pleasing compromise.

At the following meeting of Art Praxis, only three out of twenty students brought nothing into class, which is to say that seventeen students took the assignment literally. Delia went first, standing in front of the room at Mr Acconci's urging. During her valiant attempt to explain the large zero she'd made by bending a coat hanger into a crooked circle, she grew flustered and giggly, finally falling silent. The zero dangled from her outstretched arm. 'Hell,' she said finally. 'I thought of it while I was getting dressed, looking in the closet for what to wear. It's just something I made at the last minute.'

If Delia thought she'd gotten off the hook by trivializing her project, she was wrong. Acconci launched into a lecture about artists who employed the materials they found all around them, no matter how ordinary or unpromising. He told us that Robert Rauschenberg had stretched his own bedding over a wooden frame and used it as a canvas, the sheets and pillow and patchwork quilt splattered with paint. According to Acconci, *Bed* had ingeniously bridged the gap between the Abstract Expressionism of the 1950s and the representation of common objects in the 1960s.

'Rauschenberg's *Bed*,' he said, 'is interesting not only as an object, but as a gesture that turns making a painting and making a bed into similar activities.' Acconci insisted that Delia's zero was 'gestural', like the quick but knowing strokes of a sumi painter who captures the lines of a bird in flight or leaves sprouting from a sprig of bamboo. 'Maybe you did throw this together at the last minute,' he told Delia while he paced back and forth, 'but suppose the value of a work of art isn't determined by the amount of time it takes the artist to make it? And what if the artist doesn't make the work himself? Take Andy Warhol for instance, whose work is made by assistants. If we eliminate time and labour as determining factors in the value of art, what are we left with as a marker of value? The artist's intention? The artist's idea? Or perhaps art no longer has a value as we once understood the term, but rather a significance that is always changing. Your response to the assignment addresses several important issues.'

Delia's arm had fallen to her side. 'Whatever,' she said.

Next, Carl Tornquist lumbered to his feet. He cupped in his palms a handful of shredded paper and explained that it was a letter he'd been writing to his girlfriend, Cindy, but tore to pieces when words failed him. No matter how often he'd tried to write her, he couldn't think of what to say or how to say it. In fact, he hadn't written to her in so long that he wasn't sure Cindy was still his girlfriend or if she even lived at the same address. He stared into his hands and began to drone on and on about their relationship. Fortunately, Mr Acconci stopped him and wrestled the subject back to art. 'Take a pointillist's daubs of paint,' he said, 'or the splatters of Abstract Expressionism; what are these if not a record of energy and passion, not unlike a shredded letter?'

Carl continued to stare into his hands and floated, morose, back to his seat.

Finally it was my turn to stand in front of the class. I gripped the plastic pouch and gave what I'm sure was a rambling explanation of my project. All the while, Acconci nodded thoughtfully. Then it came time to enact the idea. He asked for a volunteer from the audience, as if he were a magician and I his assistant. When it became clear that the class was too abashed to respond, Acconci suggested I demonstrate the assignment myself.

Like many gay men, I understood at an early age that a fey gesture or tone of voice could put me in harm's way, and so I'd developed, in the presence of strangers, an acute self-consciousness that both protected me and produced a clammy anguish. As I lit the candle, sweat dampened my forehead and blood throbbed in my ears. Before

I knew what I was doing, I held the match to the paper instead of holding the paper above the flame, skipping the step where the secret was revealed. A couple of people muttered when they realized what I'd done wrong, but by then it was too late; the secret ignited with a quiet whoosh. When the fire grazed my fingers I quickly let go, a few black cinders drifting to the floor.

Only then did I realize what I'd been hoping for all along: Vito Acconci would take one look at my piece, proclaim me his peer and insist that his dealer exhibit my work. A one-man show remained my greatest ambition, the event toward which I aimed my days; it carried far more symbolic weight than my bar mitzvah (I'd memorized the Hebrew phonetically and gave a flat, perfunctory performance for which I was rewarded with, among other gifts, a bottle opener in the shape of Israel, the Dead Sea a hole for prying off the cap). No, a one-man show was the rite of passage that would change my life, rectify years of anomie and assure my appearance in *Life* magazine. At a gallery I'd become a man, not a rabbi or Talmud in sight.

But there I was in front of the class, the prospect of a solo show receding yet again. Acconci said something about embracing mistakes. 'Look at it this way,' he said. 'Because it went unread by a stranger, the secret retains its mystery even after it's been destroyed.' As his thoughts began to percolate, he paced the floor. 'In fact, by basing a work of art on destruction, you've challenged one of our most basic assumptions: that art is created. And because of its impermanence, your piece opposes the principle that art must be timeless instead of timely.' In one fell swoop my blunder was forgiven, my wrong made right. Acconci had found a way to aggrandize my project's vague, accidental virtues, and although I hadn't exactly set out to achieve the effects he praised me for, I had no problem basking in his praise. 'We're living in a period of history where the meanings of art have been shaken to the core. There's very little an artist can take for granted any more. Every rule is open to disagreement. Every aesthetic leads to doubt.' He stopped pacing and turned to face me. 'That should make you very happy.'

The rest of my classes at SVA were studio courses that involved time-consuming assignments like rendering the same bowl of fruit from six different angles, or making a colour chart by mixing fifty distinct gradations from the palest to the darkest blue. Unlike Art Praxis, these classes were conducted by rote and rarely deviated from the syllabus. In all fairness to those who taught them, their pedagogical point was to help improve a student's technique rather than to alter his concept of art. Still, I'd been given a new standard on which to judge instruction; if the class didn't wrench me in a new and unexpected direction, it didn't seem all that interesting.

Before becoming a conceptual artist, Vito Acconci had been a poet who was perhaps best known for his ode to the world's fastest typist, Claire Washington. 'Typist' is a manic scattering of verse that is both ironic and laudatory when it comes to Ms Washington and her nimble digits. I wasn't surprised to discover that Acconci had been a poet; his classroom spiels were abrupt and bardic. The previous year I'd read *The Contemporary American Poets*, edited by Donald Hall, for a senior English elective; awed by Anthony Hecht and Elizabeth Bishop and Sylvia Plath, my reverence for poets now shone on Acconci. Because his verbal improvisations teased meaning from art, I began to understand that thoughts, and the words that embodied them, were a clean, incisive medium. Conceptual art didn't require the mess of paint, the expense of a large studio, nor any number of the technical skills I might never master. Since an idea could be plucked more or less directly from one's imagination, conceptualism was the perfect art form for someone as impatient (and lazy) as myself.

None of us in Art Praxis was aware that our instructor was fast making his reputation as one of the most influential artists of the era. Having tried his hand at both fiction and poetry, Acconci discovered that he didn't want to represent the world on the page so much as he wanted to actively participate in it by way of language or, in the case of *Running Tape*, to document his movement through it by counting out loud.

Piqued as I was on that first day of class, *Running Tape* is a fairly methodical work of art, one that holds few surprises once the listener understands its premise. Far more provocative and unpredictable were the pieces that came in its wake. In one, Acconci chose a random stranger from a group of passers-by and then followed that person block by block, keeping his distance and stopping only after he or she entered the private domain of an office or apartment, at which point the piece was over for the day. Acconci carried out this project for an entire month, sometimes boarding buses to outlying boroughs or patronizing restaurants he'd never been to, and in one instance buying a theatre ticket and watching a matinee. He enlisted photographer Betty Johnson to take shots of him trailing after his subjects – though the artist himself was as much the subject as the people he pursued.

The stalkerish aspect of *Following Piece* is obvious, but undercut by the fact that the artist surrendered his will to the people he followed, or, more accurately, who led him on a chase. Their errands became his. Their schedules, his. He never intruded on their privacy because they had no idea they were participating in a work of art (assuming they would have considered it as such). It was they who set the artwork's pace, who determined its direction and created its shape. The voyeuristic impulse behind *Following Piece* is, after all, the voyeurism common to countless films, novels, paintings and plays – an unfamiliar life observed, its imperatives made visible.

A subsequent piece went even further in blurring the line between public and private. For *Seedbed*, Acconci had a false floor built inside the Sonnabend Gallery's main room. Every day for eight hours, he entered the crawlspace and lay there waiting, his pants pulled down around his ankles. When a visitor walked in, unawares, the artist began to masturbate while verbalizing sexual fantasies based on the footsteps he heard overhead – heavy or light, rapid or suddenly brought to a standstill – a microphone amplifying his voice through two speakers placed in the far corners of the otherwise empty room. 'You're pushing your cunt down on my mouth,' he'd murmur, or 'You're ramming your cock down into my ass.'

I never saw the piece first-hand; *Seedbed* had ended its three-week run by the time I heard about it. Besides, I'm not sure I could have mustered the courage to go even if I'd had the chance. I liked the idea that he'd found a direct and confrontational way to transform his desires into art, but I was perfectly happy to let him do the dirty work, so to speak, when it came to making sexual desire public. Had it been me hidden beneath that floor, I would have gone mute.

It wouldn't be an oversimplification to say that, while I lived in New York, my infatuation with art and my paralysis regarding sex existed in inverse proportion. My response to art was quick, metabolic and revelatory, while my response to sex was a muddle of delayed reactions and missed libidinal signals.

I've come to see myself in those days as a sort of idiot savant, a boy who could fix a broken clock yet couldn't tell the time. Many of my high-school friends had lost their virginity by then, and some, I learned from letters, had found lovers at college. Of course, my heterosexual classmates had a pervasive culture from which even the most prim and thick-headed among them could extrapolate a few helpful clues when it came to dating or getting laid.

I was so inhibited, in fact, that losing my virginity might have taken even longer had I not been visited during my freshman semester by Allison Howard, my high school's self-proclaimed nymphomaniac. Tall and blonde and perpetually tan, Allison's goal was to taste mankind in all his shapes and flavours. She'd 'had' almost every eligible boy in our twelfth-grade class, and I worried that my peers were beginning to wonder why I wasn't among her conquests. One side effect of high-school graduation was finally being free of the pressure to bed her. And then she simply showed up during one of her visits to New York, knocking on my apartment door and proposing we go out for an Indian dinner.

The restaurant reeked of sandalwood incense. Ragas whirled and eddied in the air. Instead of sitting across from me, Allison swept into the same side of the booth, prodding me along the seat with her hip until I bumped the wall.

'Don't you like to face the other person?' I asked her.

'I'd rather feel them while I eat,' she said. 'Did I mention that I'm famished?'

When we talked, I had to twist my neck at an uncomfortable angle and stare into her eyes, intrusively blue. Sometimes her head veered so close I could feel my eyes begin to cross as they strained to focus.

Kissing was as much accident as effort, since our lips were practically touching anyway. As far as I was concerned, our proximity was distracting and unnatural, about as romantic as viewing someone's pores through a magnifying glass. If I leaned to one side in order to get a little air, she'd lean too, maintaining the intimate inch between us, her warm breath bathing my face. Soon, the mechanics of fornication began to seem like less of a physical challenge than our seating arrangement. This suited my date just fine; Allison acted as though our having sex that night was a foregone conclusion. She not-so-tenderly nibbled my ear, radiant with the assurance that she could not only guess but grant my every erotic wish. Allison possessed enough desire for both of us, and if I wasn't actually excited by the prospect of having sex with her (which, after all, had seemed imminent throughout high school) her avidity threw my doubts into doubt. By the time the waiter arrived to take our order, the opportunity of a lifetime had literally thrown itself into my lap, and the easiest thing to do was give in.

When I confessed that I'd never had Indian food, Allison grabbed the menu out of my hand and ordered for us. She asked if I preferred the meal spicy or mild, then ordered it spicy anyway. The waiter grinned at her culinary daring.

During incendiary courses of saag paneer and shrimp vindaloo, Allison kneaded my thigh with one hand while she fed me forkfuls of food with the other. Spices ignited the fuse of my tongue. My eyes were wet as though from emotion. She poured glass after glass of beer from a pitcher, and I guzzled them with gratitude. Every now and then, a certain flavour made me moan. Allison's strategy, it seemed, was to get foreplay over with during the main course, thereby making an after-dinner fuck as inevitable as a mint or a toothpick.

And so it was. Back at my apartment, our skin still smelled of curry, our breath of beer. Her tongue was surprisingly agile and cool. She cupped her breasts and lifted them toward me as if to say, Look what I'm giving you! For whole moments I loved the girl for her sheer insistence, for guiding me inside her, for being too hell-bent on her own pleasure to notice I was a novice in bed. She's the one who did the fucking. I could feel the slippery muscles of her cunt, firm as a handshake, and perhaps for her as routine a greeting. If my kisses grew too eager, she'd roll on top and wrest control, shoving my limbs wherever she wanted.

In the aftermath of lovemaking, Allison wiped herself and tossed me the washcloth. I felt manly when I caught it, and thought of all the catches I'd fumbled on a field. She reached high into the sleeves of her sweater, letting it shimmy down around her. The formalities of brushing her hair and reapplying her lipstick were executed with a haste that might have been insulting had she not been so graceful, a woman practised at fleeing the scene. 'This apartment's so bare,' she told me, standing at the door and looking around. 'Like no one lives here.' She insisted on walking herself to the subway, and raised her hand to stop me when I made a move to rise.

After she shut the door behind her, I sprawled on the bed, spent from erotic accomplishment, a man who belonged in the world at last. The traffic on 12th was unusually quiet, the couple next door in a lull between sieges. It only took moments to fall asleep, and at some point during the night I found myself lying on a desolate stretch of highway instead of in my bed. An air horn blared in the distance as faintly and sweetly as a lone bird, and the next thing I knew I was crushed beneath a truck. I awoke bolt upright, distraught not only because I'd been mashed to a pulp, but because of the fact that I'd lost my virginity and then dreamed I'd been run over by a truck. What ridiculously overt symbolism on the part of my subconscious! Did the truck represent Allison? The highway my fate? Did I think of my virginity as roadkill, for God's sake? Despite my rite of passage into manhood, the world still barrelled relentlessly forward while I was left dazed in the middle of the road.

The next morning as I walked to school, the men I saw were just as tempting as they had been the day before. ■

THE DAMNED AND THE BEAUTIFUL

PATAGONIA WITHOUT DAMS

Brigitte Grignet

Aysén, Chile, is one of the most remote and undisturbed areas in the world. In 2011, the Chilean government approved the HydroAysén project – five dams and hydroelectric plants on the Baker and Pascua Rivers. The dams would irreversibly alter the ecosystem, flooding ranching land and ancestral homes and damaging a traditional way of life.

The energy from the plants would travel to Santiago over a transmission line that requires some 1,600 kilometres of forest to be cleared. This line still needs to be approved.

Life is difficult in this region. The main road that serves the area, the Carretera Austral, is mostly unpaved. Many people don't have electricity. In the countryside, men live alone, while women and children stay in small towns so that the children can go to school. They are reunited during the school holidays. This is when I visited them, when families are together on their farms.

Cochrane, the only town for miles around, would serve as a base for HydroAysén if the line is approved. About four thousand workers would have to be brought in, doubling the population of the province. Sixty kilometres south of Cochrane, the rural community of Los Ñadis is in danger of ending up at the bottom of a reservoir.

Aysén has a unique culture, a mix of Tehuelche roots and pioneer spirit. Lilli, one of my subjects, said: 'There is no land like ours.' ∎

LOOKING FOR MORE?

GRANTA

THE MAGAZINE OF NEW WRITING

SUBSCRIPTION FORM FOR US, CANADA AND LATIN AMERICA

Yes, I would like to take out a subscription to *Granta*.

GUARANTEE: If I am ever dissatisfied with my *Granta* subscription, I will simply notify you, and you will send me a complete refund or credit my credit card, as applicable, for all un-mailed issues.

YOUR DETAILS

MR / MISS / MRS / DR ....

NAME ....

ADDRESS ....

....

CITY... STATE ....

ZIP CODE .... COUNTRY ....

EMAIL ....

☐ Please check this box if you do not wish to receive special offers from *Granta*

☐ Please check this box if you do not wish to receive offers from organizations selected by *Granta*

YOUR PAYMENT DETAILS

1 year subscription: ☐ US: $48 ☐ Canada: $56 ☐ Latin America: $68

3 year subscription: ☐ US: $120 ☐ Canada: $144 ☐ Latin America: $180

Enclosed is my check for $ _____ made payable to *Granta*.

Please charge my: ☐ Visa ☐ MasterCard ☐ Amex

Card No. ☐☐☐☐☐☐☐☐☐☐☐☐☐☐☐☐

Exp. ☐☐☐☐

Security Code ☐☐☐☐☐

SIGNATURE .... DATE ....

Please mail this order form with your payment instructions to:

Granta Publications
PO Box 359
Congers, NY 10920-0359

Or call 845-267-3031
Or visit GRANTA.COM for details

Source code: BUS126PM

A KILLING

Katherine Faw Morris

COY HAWKINS STANDS BEHIND NIKKI WITH HIS ARMS LAID OVER HER ARMS, HIS HANDS CUPPING HER HANDS, HIS FINGERS ON TOP OF HER FINGERS. As they pull the trigger he rams his shoulder into her shoulder.

'Don't flinch.'

He lets go of her. He picks up his beer and points with it.

'Go ahead,' Coy Hawkins says.

Nikki raises the gun at the big house again.

SHE WATCHES HIM PUSH A BRUSH THROUGH THE BARREL. She watches him drop oil on a rag and shine the black metal. The parts fit back together in hard snaps and the magazine clicks in last. He wipes his hands on a rag.

'The first time's the worst,' Coy Hawkins says.

'I done it before,' Nikki says.

He cuts his eyes to her.

'Wesley Harrell,' she says.

Coy Hawkins points his clean gun at one of the walls of the kitchen.

'Oh yeah,' he says.

SHE LOOKS AT HIM. She is startled by the bandanna around his face. A second ago he wasn't wearing it. He pulls up his hood. He nods at her.

She knocks on an apartment door, the welfare apartments in town that are grey and wooden and drop down to the riverbank.

When the peephole darkens she takes one step back. The door catches on its chain.

'Hey,' Nikki says.

A man stares at her.

'Who are you?'

'Nikki,' she says.

'Who?'

'Can I use your phone?'

'What?' he says.

Nikki holds up Coy Hawkins's cell.

'Mine's dead.'

The man's eyes flick up and down. Nikki smiles at him. She's wearing a dress with see-through parts. Her cat's eyes are slightly crooked but her lips are very red.

Nikki jams her knee inside and touches his. He's older than Coy Hawkins. His cheeks are cut by two deep lines.

'Hold up,' he says.

As soon as he slams the door Nikki takes two steps back, and when he opens it again, wide, unchained, Coy Hawkins pivots off the outside wall and slugs a baseball bat into the man's gut.

'What the fuck,' the man grunts.

She crawls underneath the man while Coy Hawkins smashes him over the back.

No one's in the living room. She turns a right for the kitchen like Coy Hawkins said. The other man, the important one, is sitting at a table. His name is Lee Church. He is nothing like she pictured him. She raises the gun and surges at him.

'Drugs and cash,' Nikki says.

He looks surprised.

'Drugs and cash.'

He just sits there. She starts to panic. She hears Coy Hawkins's bat behind her. She stomps her high heel on the linoleum and lets out a little shriek.

'Are you stupid? This is a motherfucking stick-up.'

Lee Church puts his cigarette in an ashtray and then he puts his hands up.

THEY'RE PULLED OFF IN THE WOODS, OUT IN THE COUNTY. Coy Hawkins has a Ziploc bag of cocaine in his lap. Nikki has rubber-banded bills between her feet. That went well, Nikki thinks.

'Don't use your real name next time,' Coy Hawkins says.

'Why not?' Nikki says.

He dips the pickup key in the Ziploc. He looks at her. In the overhead light his face is like wax.

'Bump?' he says.

COKE SMELLS COLD AND CHEMICAL LIKE THE INSIDE OF A REFRIGERATOR. It's what back then smells like, now when she thinks of it. Nikki takes a drag off Coy Hawkins's Kool and its blast of menthol is the best thing that's ever been in her mouth.

The interstate reels out. The sign says thirty miles to Charlotte. Coy Hawkins has called somebody on his phone. It's not really dead. This time he's going to sell, Nikki thinks. She is giddy and she can't feel her teeth.

They have already passed over the service road. They have already passed over the gorilla pimp. They could be going anywhere.

SHE LOOKS AROUND ALERTLY. She sniffs drip up her nose.

'Where are we?' Nikki says.

'Kannapolis,' Coy Hawkins says.

'Where?'

On both sides of a wide street every house is the same. They glow up in the headlights of the pickup, white and sagging. After a while Coy Hawkins stops in front of one.

A Mexican man opens the door.

'Where the fuck you been?' he says.

Coy Hawkins shrugs.

'Trying to stay out of trouble, man.'

Nikki follows him in. The house's living room is strewn with little girls' toys. There's a blow-up castle in the middle of it. Coy Hawkins and the man go into what must be the kitchen. They close a bed sheet behind them.

'You can't go in there.'

Nikki looks at her. The little girl is curled on the couch, holding a baby doll and wearing a tutu. She is five or six. Nikki puts her hands on her hips.

'Why not?'

'You're not supposed to,' the little girl says.

'Why?' Nikki says.

'Because you're a girl.'

'What?'

Nikki thinks she sees the little girl smirk.

'My mom can't even go in there,' the little girl says.

Her tutu is much pinker than Nikki's hair used to be. Nikki kicks a Barbie Corvette out of the way of her feet.

'Hey,' the little girl says.

Nikki sits beside her.

'My mama's dead,' Nikki says.

The little girl makes a face.

'She killed herself,' Nikki says.

The little girl drops her mouth on the doll's head.

It's probably four in the morning. They watch TV. Nikki doesn't understand because it's in Spanish.

'She left me when I was a baby,' Nikki says.

She doesn't know why she just said that. She smells something like burning ketchup.

'You smell that?'

The little girl says nothing. Nikki looks at the bed sheet.

'What is it?'

'Papi,' the little girl says.

Nikki stands up and the girl cuts her eyes from the TV. For a second they stare at each other. The little girl is not going to be as pretty as her. If she touched the little girl she would be gooey, Nikki thinks. Nikki sits down again.

When the bed sheet opens Coy Hawkins is carrying a different grocery bag than the one he came in with. He snaps his fingers at Nikki.

'My daughter,' Coy Hawkins says.

The man looks at her briefly.

'HOW MUCH DID YOU GET FOR IT?'

'Half a ki of heroin,' Coy Hawkins says.

Nikki's eyes dart to the bag between her feet.

'What?'

On the way home they stop and buy party balloons.

THE HEROIN IS BLACK. It's sticky. It's shiny.

'What's wrong with it?'

'Nothing,' Coy Hawkins says.

They're in the kitchen. They're sitting at the card table. Coy Hawkins has ripped open the bag of party balloons.

'It ain't white,' Nikki says.

'It's black tar.'

'It's what?'

'Mexican shit,' Coy Hawkins says.

He breaks off a tarry black chunk.

'You got everybody up here snorting pills and paying what?'

Nikki shrugs. Coy Hawkins answers his own question.

'A dollar a milligram. Eighty dollars for one fucking 80,' he says.

He nudges the black chunk onto a balloon's head. He turns the balloon inside out, knots it, pushes it through so that it's right side out, and knots it again. He holds it up.

'How much you think this costs?'

'I don't know,' Nikki says.

'Ten dollars.'

'What?'

He clips it to a scale and hangs it before him.

'Tenth of a gram,' he says.

He tosses it to her.

'Whoever brings this shit up here first is gonna make a killing.'

Nikki just stares at him.

'I'm trying to teach you something,' Coy Hawkins says.

She is not paying attention. She is thinking about how much better it would be if the table were covered in cash. She looks at the black lump. It doesn't even seem like that much. Her jaw is still going from that one bump.

'Pills are the same as heroin?'

Coy Hawkins laughs.

'Yeah,' he says.

The balloon is blue. It's tiny. Nikki looks at it again.

SHE YAWNS. When she stumbles into the kitchen a man and a woman are sitting there. They turn to her. Then they turn to Coy Hawkins.

'It's cool,' he says.

He has a roll of tinfoil.

He tears off a sheet. He quarters it and rips it into squares. He burns the side of one piece with his lighter. He sticks heroin to the other side. He wraps another square around a pen and pushes it out to make a straw.

He holds up the heroin foil. He flicks his lighter under it. There is a long crackling as he pulls up smoke. He lifts his head with the straw between his lips. He blows out and the whole kitchen explodes in burning ketchup.

Nikki leans against a wall.

Coy Hawkins fixes a second foil and passes it to the woman.

'See how it slides. Chase it,' he says.

The woman waves her hand.

'I smoked Oxys before,' she says.

'That's the stupidest thing I ever heard,' Coy Hawkins says.

She looks insulted but when Coy Hawkins flicks the lighter she lowers her head.

The man peers over the woman's shoulder. When the woman has a coughing fit the man takes the foil from her and lights it for himself.

'Shooting's better,' Coy Hawkins says.

He shivers.

'You get that rush.'

The woman shakes her head.

'I don't fuck with needles.'

'You'll get over it,' Coy Hawkins says.

'How much?' the man says.

Coy Hawkins throws out a handful of balloons.

'Tell your friends,' he says.

The man is picking up the balloons that fell on the floor. He's stuffing his socks with them. Nikki feels light. She watches the burnt-ketchup smoke settle onto everything, onto a missed patch of hair on the man's shaved head.

Nikki drops her foot on a yellow one. She curls her toes over it. The man looks at her. He narrows his eyes. She glares back at him.

'What?' she says.

The man scratches his leg. He sits up.

'Fucking Coy Hawkins. In the flesh,' he says.

NIKKI SITS ON THE BATHROOM FLOOR TO CONCENTRATE. Smoking heroin's harder than it looks.

She burns herself. Her mouth fills with bitter, vinegary smoke and she coughs. The heroin slides in a brown streak over the lit foil and she chases it. Finally it stops rolling. It blackens and pops.

She leans against the shower with the straw in her mouth. She feels nothing.

SHE PUKES IN THE TOILET.

NIKKI WANDERS INTO THE KITCHEN. There are different men and women. She's never seen them before.

She wants something to kill the taste in her mouth. She stands in the open refrigerator staring. A man asks her something and before she can answer asks her something else.

'What?' Nikki says.

She feels a pinch on her arm and after she turns around she sees Coy Hawkins. She looks at him like she would anyone. She doesn't even care.

'You seen that other roll of tinfoil?' he says.

'What?' Nikki says.

She is made of air.

'Go sit on the couch,' Coy Hawkins says.

On the couch Nikki scratches up and down her shins. She scratches her arms. She scratches her neck. She scratches especially behind her knees, the backs of her hands just brushing the plaid of the cushions, and murmurs to herself.

She's itchy like she's been snorting pills but heroin is a real drug. Real drugs are a secret. Nikki has always loved secrets. Back then was full of them.

Nikki blinks at the TV. She sees her palms open in her lap. Bewildered she looks all around the living room but there's no one there.

Her head droops again. Her eyes close. It's okay, she thinks, everything.

ON HEROIN SHE DREAMS. She dreams a wild dream she can't control. Mostly a mutant tries to eat her. Nikki snaps awake.

IN THE KITCHEN COY HAWKINS IS TALKING TO A MAN. Nikki stands there a second.

'Plus it's more cost-effective, shooting it,' Coy Hawkins says.

'We're gonna make a killing,' Nikki says.

They both look at her.

'What?' Coy Hawkins says.

'Us.'

Nikki says this only to him. Coy Hawkins puts his fingers up to his lips.

'We're gonna bring this shit up here first and it's gonna be like back then. You're gonna be the biggest in the county again.'

Coy Hawkins stares at her. Then he drops his hand from his mouth and starts laughing. The man looks at Coy Hawkins. He starts laughing, too.

NIKKI WASHES HER HAIR. She shaves everywhere. She brushes her teeth and spits out blood in the sink.

She opens the cabinet underneath. She pulls out the hairdryer and flat iron and the whole pouch of make-up.

She looks at her face in the mirror. She does not see a stupid little girl.

SHE HAS TO WALK ALMOST ALL THE WAY DOWN TO THE BOTTOM ROAD BEFORE SHE GETS RECEPTION ON COY HAWKINS'S PHONE.

'its nikki. hey' she texts.

She drops the grocery bag between her feet. She keeps looking over her shoulder. The phone lights up.

'what?' Wesley texts.

'i wanna see u' Nikki texts.

'why'

'??'

Nikki rolls her eyes.

'just come get me im at my dads'

'u owe me' Wesley texts.

Her pulse picks up.

WESLEY LOCKS AND CHAINS THE CAMPER DOOR. It's just the two of them. Nikki peeks around the curtain at the air mattress to make sure.

'Where's old girl?' Nikki says.

'What do you want?' Wesley says.

Her hair is huge. She's wearing the best of the dresses and she's brought balloons. When she dumps out the grocery bag onto Wesley's table ten or so tumble out.

Wesley comes close to her. He chins at the table without breaking his stare.

'What the fuck is that?'

'Black tar heroin,' Nikki says.

He grabs her by the back of the neck. He slams her forehead to her knees.

'Quit it,' she shrieks.

'You wearing a fucking wire?'

'No, get off me.'

'Where the fuck you get it?'

'From my daddy, where you think?'

Wesley pulls his hand out of her dress. He lets go and she shoves him in the chest.

'Asshole,' Nikki says.

She slouches back on the couch. Wesley sits down beside her and picks up a balloon. He weighs it in his palm.

'It's the same as pills.'

'Yeah, I know,' Wesley says.

'Except it's way cheaper and better,' Nikki says.

'You done it?'

Nikki kicks under the table at the bag of Mama's clothes.

'Yeah,' she says.

Wesley gets up. He steps around the table. He opens some drawers. He steps back with a roll of tinfoil.

'Right?' he says.

'It's better if you shoot it,' Nikki says.

She shivers.

'You get that rush.'

Wesley kind of laughs. He sits down and opens the balloon with his teeth. He tears off a piece of foil and smudges the heroin onto it and it gleams.

'No,' Nikki says.

'What?' Wesley says.

'You're doing it wrong.'

'I'm doing it wrong?'

'You gotta burn off the shiny side.'

'Why?'

205

'Because.'

Nikki sighs. She unfolds her arms and takes the foil from him.

'You gotta pen?' she says.

She shows him.

She makes a straw. She fixes a foil and lights it. As the heroin rolls she chases it. She lifts her head with smoke in her mouth and Wesley's eyes glint.

'What?'

Wesley shakes his head.

'Nothing,' he says.

She makes one for him. She stares at his bent head while he smokes it. Like this is hard, Nikki thinks.

'You heard about Lee Church?' Nikki says.

'What?'

Wesley's coughing.

'Lee Church. He stays in them Glenhaven apartments.'

Wesley blows burnt-ketchup smoke out of the side of his mouth.

'I heard he got robbed.'

Nikki gathers all her hair to one side. She pulls her fingers through it and tilts her head and looks at him.

'By a couple Mexicans,' Wesley says.

'Mexicans?'

He's looking at the foil straw.

'No, it wasn't,' Nikki says.

'I heard it from Lee Church himself. The fucking cartel,' Wesley says.

THERE ARE THREE OR FOUR STRANGE CARS IN THE YARD.

On the couch there are strange people nodding out.

'Where the fuck you been?'

Coy Hawkins leans out of the kitchen.

'Like you care,' Nikki says.

She goes down the hall. She slams the bathroom door as hard as she can.

LATER SHE SEES HIM GO INTO THE BEDROOM. She goes after him. His hair is wet and in the mirrored closet he's combing it. Nikki sits on the bed, watching him.

'Lee Church is telling everybody it was two Mexicans that robbed him,' she says.

'So what?' Coy Hawkins says.

'So why would he say that?'

In the mirror Coy Hawkins's eyes shift to her.

'Why do you think?' Coy Hawkins says.

Behind him Nikki looks at herself. Then she looks at the green carpet. It's so ugly, she thinks. She shoves her toes into it. She crosses her arms over her chest.

'You think I'm just bait,' she says.

'No,' he says.

He turns and looks at her. He grips the towel around his waist by its knot. She stares at Mama's name on him. It's almost gone, too. He throws his comb on the bed and holds his hand out.

'Give me my phone back,' he says.

Later still a man walks in on her in the bathroom. She rips her dress down but he just stands there. She doesn't know what to do. She nearly hisses at him.

'Get out,' Nikki says.

The man leans against the wall on one hand.

'Calm down,' he says.

She wiggles out under his arm.

'IS THERE A NIKKI HERE?' A WOMAN SAYS.

From the couch Nikki glares.

'Yeah. What?' she says.

The woman starts scratching her arm. She closes her eyes.

'Some guy's looking for you,' the woman says.

In the yard is Wesley. Nikki freezes on the trailer's top step. She thinks about calling Coy Hawkins. But Wesley's alone this time. He's looking around at the other cars.

'What happened to my ride?' Wesley says.

Luckily she hasn't changed. The best of the dresses laces up the sides.

'We didn't want it no more,' she says.

She reties two bows.

'What are you doing up here?'

Wesley puts his hands in his pockets and shrugs.

'I wanna buy an ounce,' he says.

Nikki tries to hide her grin but can't. She opens the trailer door and looks over her shoulder.

She kicks everybody out of the kitchen. Then she shuts the accordion door. She grabs a beer from the refrigerator and cracks it and sets it on the card table in front of him.

Wesley tilts back in his chair and crosses his arms behind his head.

'Where's Coy Hawkins?' he says.

'Why?' Nikki says.

He looks at her. She puts her hands on her hips.

'Just one, right?' she says.

Wesley laughs. He lets his chair bang the floor. He takes the cigarette from behind his ear and sticks it in his mouth.

'Wait here,' Nikki says.

She goes into the bedroom where the bigger chunks are stashed. They're stuffed in the toes of Coy Hawkins's boots and wrapped in cut-up grocery bags. She pulls one out. Coy Hawkins is lying on the bed.

'What are you doing?' he says.

'Selling an ounce to Wesley Harrell.'

She nearly bounces back to the kitchen. She closes the accordion door behind her. She tosses the chunk on the card table.

'One piece,' Nikki says.

Wesley stubs his cigarette out.

'That's what you call heroin ounces,' she says.

'Okay,' he says.

He has his own scale. He pulls it out like a gun. Nikki perches on the chair across from him. She puts her face in her hand.

He takes the chunk off the scale.

'It's short,' he says.

He puts it on again.

'It's twenty-five.'

'I know,' Nikki says.

Wesley looks at her.

'There's twenty-eight grams in an ounce,' he says.

'It's heroin weight.'

'What?'

'It's a Mexican ounce,' Nikki says.

'A what?'

Nikki racks her brain for all the other things Coy Hawkins has said.

'It's the metric system, dumb ass,' Coy Hawkins says.

Nikki flicks her head. He's standing with one arm folding open the accordion door. After a second Wesley nods at him.

'Makes sense,' Wesley says.

He reaches in his pocket and then he looks at Coy Hawkins.

'How much, man?' he says.

Wesley's beer is still where Nikki put it. She picks it up and hurls it at the wall.

SHE STALKS DOWN THE HALL. In the bedroom she bangs the door behind them. Coy Hawkins goes over to the bed and sits on it. He looks up at her.

'That's my money,' she says.

He counts out half the twenties and pushes them across the mattress.

'You need to be careful,' he says.

'Of what?' Nikki says.

Coy Hawkins shakes his head. He snaps towards the kitchen.

'Go clean up that mess.'

NIKKI TUCKS THE STRAW BEHIND HER EAR. She smiles at herself. Her pupils are the tiny heads of pins. Her eyes are the bluest blue. She reaches up and rests her arms on top of her head and she can count all her ribs in the bathroom mirror.

She thinks she looks great. But her hair is brownish again. Under the sink is a bleach kit.

When she comes out the trailer's dark. She wants to show someone. She finds him in the living room. He's stretched out in his chair. She turns on the floor lamp and grins.

'You like it?' Nikki says.

Coy Hawkins squints at her. He feels for his cigarettes.

'Not really,' he says.

THERE IS A MAN WITH A NEEDLE. Nikki watches him.

He pushes the black tar out of a balloon and into a bottle cap. He adds a splash of water and burns his lighter underneath. The bottle cap is metal. The heroin starts to bubble.

He pulls the head off a Q-tip. He drops the cotton in the cap and pushes it around with the needle tip. He pulls the plunger up with his teeth.

He has a rubber tie like a nurse. He yanks it around the woman's arm. Big green veins stand up when he slaps her. He rubs his thumb over one.

He jabs the needle in and then he wiggles it some. Blood blooms into the syringe. Slowly he pushes the plunger until all the black-red liquid runs in.

Nikki watches the woman's head fall to her chest and stay there like it's broken. Nikki sits down in the other chair. She puts her arm on the card table.

'Do me,' she says.

The man stares at her.

'Ain't this your daddy's place?' he says.

Nikki shrugs.

'So?'

'So you're how old?'

Nikki stares back at him.

'Sixteen,' she says.

She's thirteen.

The man takes off his baseball hat and turns it around the other way. He pulls it low over his eyes.

'Shit,' he says.

He holds her arm by the wrist and tears open another balloon. She can see into the living room from her chair and down the hall to the bedroom door. She waits for Coy Hawkins to open it.

The needle pricks going in. After he slides it out Nikki's arm flares with a white-hot itch from shoulder to fingertip.

SHE CAREENS THROUGH THE DARK. She can only see the dashboard before her. She is not driving and she cannot wake up but she knows she is being chased. The road breaks.

HEROIN IS THE MOST SECRET OF THEM ALL AND NEEDLES ARE THE MOST SECRET PART AND SHE HAS ALWAYS LOVED SECRETS EVER SINCE SHE WAS A LITTLE GIRL.

SHE DREAMS THAT COY HAWKINS IS STRANGLING HER. She goes into the bathroom to look at her neck and there is a purple ring around her throat. She is overcome with the feeling that her skin is quivering three inches from the rest of her and if she touched it it would give like a sponge. It's a fat girl's neck that doesn't belong to her. She has to squat down to keep from puking. A loud noise jerks her up. She is awake. She is sitting in the kitchen chair.

'Damn, she looks like she just got her wings,' somebody says.

COY HAWKINS IS SITTING IN THE OTHER CHAIR. Where the man used to be. He's looking at her arm. Nikki looks at it, too. There's dried blood in the crook of her elbow.

She blinks at him. She thinks she sees something flicker across his face before he goes back to looking at her like always.

'You're fucking up.'

He says this and gets up. ■

OFF THE ROAD

Andrew Brown

'Don't climb on behind him,' said Paula. 'It's knicker-wetting, and not in the good way.' Bryan laughed and revved the bike. I climbed on. 'I love these walls,' he said. 'They ripple most agreeably in the light.'

The outbuildings of his father's farm looked stable enough to me, but then he gunned the engine and I had to grab hard at the rails beneath my seat as the speed pushed us back, and we lurched forwards, then down to the left. A brief glimpse of tarmac rushed past, and I clung on as the bike rocked and dipped, tugging at me inside a ferocious noise. That uneven plaster on the wall was the last firm surface I saw until the ride ended and we were back in the yard where we had started. Now it quivered for my eyes too, and I am pretty certain that it wasn't an effect of the drugs.

Bryan always drove cars or rode his bike much too fast, whether he was drunk, drugged or freshly out of bed, but speed alone no longer frightened him enough to blot out all his other fears. 'I need so much to feel alive,' he'd say. I never quite knew whether this meant that he needed to feel alive a great deal, or that he needed a great deal of help to feel alive, and I don't suppose he did. Either way, Paula thought he was stupid to say it and told him so often: 'I feel quite alive enough,' she'd say. 'Of course I'm fucking alive. And so are you, sweetie.' She was a big Scots girl with coarse red hair bound in a ponytail and skin the colour of thin cream. Blue eyes that seemed to shift like agates underwater. She wore a biker jacket too big for her – God knows where they had found it – hanging open because the day was warm. None of us wore helmets.

Bryan looked at me with the indulgent affection he felt for everyone when he was on his bike, a seat that seemed to exalt him above particularity. Paula hated it. She didn't want to ride again. She didn't want him to ride again. 'Go on,' he said, 'one last run then we'll stop.' I urged her on as well, partly from fear that otherwise I'd have to ride again, and she agreed at last.

'After, we'll have our tea. With strawberries.' This always seemed to her the best of all the luxuries of his life. With that promise, he gunned the bike and they were off, the noise echoing down what seemed to be a tunnel of stone walls along the twisty roads towards the fell.

I sat on a straw bale and rolled a cigarette to recover. The Delauneys' farm was built around a courtyard, part brick and part rough concrete, overlaid with mud and weeds. There were barns and outbuildings round three sides: the farmhouse itself was a thick-walled whitewashed building that seemed to crouch against the wind. Bryan's family had lived there for at least three hundred years. None before him had been an artist. But his passions could set like iron, and he had decided on art college after public school. There he was admired for his talent nearly as much as for his reckless hungers. He wasted no time on anything but drawing and painting, and his drawing had extraordinary force and freshness. At a time when nothing was valued more than self-expression in art, he understood that the personality of the artist was irrelevant to his task.

By the time my cigarette was half gone the noise of the motorbike had died away into the hills and the world around me had resumed its accustomed solidity. Then my stillness was interrupted with a creak and a choked scream of protesting metal as David the stockman opened one of the barns. He was a lean figure, like an old curved stick, in a filthy Barbour jacket. He wore a cloth cap tipped down on his forehead and looked at us younger humans as though we were never as interesting as his ewes. Now he emerged leading a bay pony across the yard. When he'd let it into an adjoining field he returned for the second one, a stocky black-and-white creature.

As he did so, the noise of the bike resumed and rapidly grew. The pony grew nervous, jerking its head against the rope. The bike entered the last little section of the drive, alongside a drystone wall, and Bryan – as he always did – kicked down a gear for maximum dramatic effect. The noise rose sharply, amplified by the little wall, and the pony panicked. It tugged the rope from David's hands with the whole weight of its body and bolted straight in front of the bike as it entered the yard. Bryan hit the pony side on, and crashed onto the bricks. Paula, seated behind him, went over the top of the animal, flat in the air until she twisted around, and struck the ground on her back, head and shoulders first.

I thought she must be dead. But when I knelt beside her, her eyes held me. 'I cannae fucking move,' she said. 'Help me up.'

I seemed to be moving in an underwater silence, as after a bomb. Bryan and Paula were still on the ground, Bryan by the pony, which had been knocked over by the impact and after one terrible scream was silent. Bryan seemed to be swearing and whimpering by turns. David was with them. Paula was on her back, with a terrible earnestness in her eyes. I knelt beside her on the rough farmyard brick, holding her hand. I smelt straw and horse piss. Her jeans were soaking and dark. It wasn't blood. There was blood, though, quite a lot of it. It went on seeping across the cobbles, glistening, then viscous. Paula's head moved a little. 'Help me,' she said again.

I realized that I should go to the house and phone an ambulance but I could not move. There was Paula's hand limp in mine. I felt she should be clutching me. I wanted to be comforting. But the limp weakness of it meant I could not put it down. Still that underwater silence filled the yard, and then the sound of a smooth engine coming closer. When I looked up Colonel Delauney's green Jaguar was nosing into the yard. It stopped abruptly, without any screech of brakes. I don't remember any sound, even when he ran to his son, stooped over him briefly and then ran into the house. He came out a little later, carrying a shotgun. He stood over the pony, which was still moving feebly, and shot it twice in the head. Then he broke open the gun and came to us.

Paula had not flinched at the sound of the gunshots and lay still on the ground. 'Don't move her,' he said, and added, speaking to her at last, 'There's an ambulance coming. Rest. Be still. The bad part's over.'

He left and crossed the ruined yard to his son, crouching there for a while. I could hear nothing of what was said, and then he straightened and stood for a moment. He walked back to the house, re-emerged without the shotgun and spoke in his normal voice that carried clearly all around the yard.

'David! We must remove the pony.' They dragged the poor creature to one side before the ambulance arrived.

Bryan went in on a stretcher, but Paula – I was astonished by the care the attendants took with her, the collar they inflated round her head, the solemnity of their kindness. I don't think any of us but Colonel Delauney realized what had happened yet.

'You wait in the house, Andrew. I'll travel with them. You'll need to wash up.'

Later I sat in the chintzy downstairs living room, eyeing the sideboard. If Bryan had been there, he would have poured us both large whiskeys. I could not. Perhaps I was afraid of the Colonel. But I think I was more afraid of something which whiskey could only make worse, and by the nameless intuition that these problems would form the greater part of adult life.

The farmhouse creaked around me, settling in the evening chill. The room smelt of smoke and oak, and faintly of dog. Colonel Delauney lived alone when Bryan and his friends were not staying there; Mrs Delauney had run off five years ago with her last lover, a wealthy heart surgeon much older than she was. Delauney had remained on the farm. Maura had hated being a farmer's wife as much as she had hated being an army wife, but he had returned to the business of his family, conscientiously at first, and then with a growing kind of love, though never with the hope he'd had in soldiering.

When he returned, his back was still straight, but for the first time I had known him he looked as if this poise required muscles, not just grace, and the lines round his mouth and between his eyebrows were sharply cut. He made us both whiskeys, large, without water, and came to sit opposite me.

'They're all right,' he said. 'At least they will be. Bryan has a broken collarbone, cracked ribs and a lot of bruising. Paula – may be worse off. They're worried that she has injured her spine. We won't know for some days.'

He took a healthy swallow of the whiskey. I noticed that I had done so too, when he spoke.

'What happened? Why did he hit the pony?'

'He couldn't stop. He tried to – he almost made it.'

'But he should never have been driving so fast.'

To agree would have been disloyal but to deny it absurd. The bright boisterous cheerfulness of the afternoon was impossible to explain, and difficult even to remember now that I knew what it had led to. The silence prolonged itself, and when he spoke again it was without any edge of accusation. There was merely a sort of bewilderment that his son could have been so careless.

'David is very shocked. He had hopes for that animal. So did I.'

The fact, revealed, carried its own condemnation. I understood it as a reproach for Bryan's selfishness, and felt it as one for mine, too. It was easy, then, to overlook the thin veins of sympathy that were threaded through the Colonel's stony concepts of duty and decency; at that moment I was too consumed by my own wretchedness to admit that he might be unhappy too.

'How is Bryan feeling? How is Paula?'

'He was rather woozy and confused from all the painkillers. Not complaining, at any rate. She was asleep. I didn't try to wake her. I suppose her family must be told. Do you know how to reach them?'

'I'm not sure I have a phone number. She never spoke about them much.' In fact I was not sure her family had a phone. The town in Fife where she had come from figured quite large in the nightmare stories she told to entertain her friends. 'Buckhaven is so rough I had to take my dad as a getaway driver to visit my auntie who was threatening to sell Great-Grandma's wedding ring for drink,' she'd say. Bryan, when he had first known her, would pick the stories up and embroider them still further, creating a tapestry of alcoholic grotesques whose pastimes were theft, incest and three-card brag, all broken up by humourless violence.

Bryan, I said, would certainly have her parents' address and could write to them when he had recovered a little. Meanwhile, I should go home. But the Colonel did not want me to go. I was invited to stay until the other two came back from hospital. This was not entirely welcome, but they were my friends, and I did feel in some way responsible for what had happened. I wasn't responsible for Bryan. No one was, least of all Bryan himself. But I had urged Paula onto her last ride, and I wanted to see her well. I studied law. I wanted to do the right thing.

As our whiskeys emptied and I prepared to go to bed, the telephone rang. It lived on an oak chest in the hall outside the sitting room. Colonel Delauney thought it would have been an intrusion to allow it into a room where people might be talking, or thinking. And so, when I came to stay as Bryan's school friend, I had been used to finding his mother Maura poised there, with the receiver in her left hand and a cigarette in her right, legs crossed and elbows pressed to her sides. The impression was of a great quantity of sexual and emotional energy pressed into a container not quite large enough, so that the cigarette smoke and the high, rather breathy voice seemed like exhalations from an inner fire. Her voice would die as I approached, a friendly smile following me through the room until I was safely out of earshot.

Now, when the phone rang, Delauney rose from the sofa as if summoned to action. I followed him halfway across the room. He barked into the telephone. 'Hello? Carnwath 4478,' and then his voice dropped. 'Maura.'

His voice crumpled into a register I had never heard before, full of bruised determination, and then he looked up, saw me standing in the doorway and gestured me fiercely away. I shut the door between us, but stood for a little while listening. I could distinguish no words but his tone was apologetic in a way that I could not understand, as if he had been to blame for her running away and for her staying away, when he had always behaved quite correctly.

Delauney's rectitude had always unnerved me because I could no more live up to it than his son could, but now I was frightened. Rectitude was part of the order of our world. We were young, we failed and we were punished for it. But as I listened to the Colonel's voice stumbling, a suspicion formed, or half formed: that rectitude might after all not be enough, and that all our rebellions might not have been testing anything lasting and true. For a moment, I saw myself as a child lost on the fell as evening came, who had seen his mother cast her reassuring shadow across the field and had run towards her, only to find a stone which the setting sun had tricked out in a human shape.

When the Colonel returned he poured another whiskey for each of us and sat down. Shellfire could not have rattled him as his ex-wife's phone call had.

'Maura,' he said. 'I always found her difficult.'

After a silence, he continued.

'A "bouncy blonde", people said when I first asked about her. We'd danced, and she seemed – so alive – and then she disappeared. Just vanished from my life. Hadn't been part of the usual set at all. So I asked the man whose sister had thrown the ball, Tommy Pullinger. Good sort. He said, "Ah, yes, the bouncy blonde." She certainly bounced. She –'

I wondered what he would say. By the time she left him, Maura had bounced one way or another with almost all her husband's fellow officers.

'She bounced, you know. She bounced me like Tigger.'

This was entirely unexpected.

'I felt such a joy, you know. Like a full moon. And then, after we'd married, after Bryan was born, she turned away. And there was nothing – I felt my orbit was just carrying me – carrying me away from her. So we came here, but she was already too far away. Sometimes I think she never loved anyone. Never could. She certainly never loved Bryan.'

I gave a cautious mumble of assent. Bryan had never felt loved by his mother. Dazzled, yes. Compelled to love her and condemned to disappoint her. And this absurdly honourable old man had been left to try to love them both – a task for which nothing in his upbringing had prepared him. How much happier he'd have been charging a machine-gun nest. Now both of them had failed him.

B ryan's postcards were always proper Donald McGill ones, even then a rarity. He bought them in the less-frequented post offices of the Lake District. The first one, about six months after the crash, showed an earthy yokel standing beside a girl with a chest made from helium balloons. They were looking into a field. The punchline was: 'It's not my sheep.' There was a letter too, written on a page torn out of a notebook. His handwriting, as ever, was confident to the verge of illegibility. Maura, it seemed, was coming to visit, and he wanted my help. Paula had added a sentence, which was underlined: *Come up. I need you to put some spine into this drunken bum.*

M aura drove a gold Mercedes, the colour of her ego. You never saw cars like that on the road. In fact the only other time I had seen that colour was on the special Corgi model of James Bond's car, which had a bulletproof shield and a working ejector seat for unwanted passengers. Her hair, once quite naturally blonde, was by now a little metallic too, swinging on her shoulders when she moved.

When the car pulled up outside the cottage the three of us were there, waiting on the hard standing outside. It was a day of watery sunlight and fresh wind. Paula, when Bryan wheeled her out, had given a sigh that was almost a shudder. 'It's a day for running around,' she said.

'A day for running away is what you mean,' said Bryan.

'Oh, Maura, what a lovely day,' I said as she stepped from the car.

She quite ignored this and walked straight to Paula, stooped and kissed her on the forehead and straightened quickly. Then she looked at her more carefully.

'You're looking well. Your eyes are strong.'

She looked around at Bryan and me. When Maura was not thinking about you, her lack of attention was total.

'How lovely to see you, Mother,' said Bryan with his most disarming grin. From her he had learned, and with her he had perfected, the trick of standing always a little to one side of what he said. She kissed his cheek.

'Would you like a cup of tea?'

'I don't think so. Not if you have made it. Andrew may know about hygiene, but I'm not sure you do. I think I will take you all off to the seaside. Where is the nearest place?'

'Arnside,' said Paula before anyone else could. She had always enjoyed the seafront there.

'That sounds wonderful. I can't get you in my car, so you and Bryan show the way. I'll drive Andrew.'

'But we have tea ready. I cleared the table in your honour. I even cleaned the floor – the layer we got down to had only a few sheep's bones from the last time the Colonel feasted with his chums in here. That has to be the original floor. Any archaeologist would believe me. Why wouldn't you?'

'Bryan, I think we should do what Paula wants. And so that's what we are going to do. I came here to visit both of you, after all. Andrew, you get in the front. I want to talk to you.'

I was not used to helping with Paula's wheelchair. She had been large and yet so full of life that she never seemed to press heavily on the ground. Now my wrists hurt from lifting the handles of her chair as we levered her into the adapted cab that Bryan was now driving.

Maura's car seemed very spacious after the glimpse of darkness inside the taxi. Coming out of the drive, she stopped to light a cigarette, and then accelerated hard to catch up.

'It won't do Bryan any good to drive so cautiously now, you know,' she said, braking into formation behind him. 'So how did it happen? Why is he doing this? Christ, is he going to get God next?'

She looked at the road ahead, leaving a little smoke hanging under the rear-view mirror.

'I don't think he's going to get God, Maura. God did this to Paula, remember? If she hadn't landed the way she did, nothing would have happened.'

'And if Auntie had balls, she'd be my uncle.' She giggled at her own joke.

'No, really. I actually think what happened was just bad luck. That's all it was. No one could have foreseen it. No one knew that David would be bringing the pony across the yard. He had no idea Bryan was coming back.'

'But any fool could have seen that playing around with bikes on a drunken afternoon would make an accident likely.'

'Maura, that's not fair. Everyone lives like that around here. You know that.'

'Yes. That's one reason I left. The imbecility of rural life.'

As she dismissed the wreckage she had left behind her, I felt for a moment something of the Colonel's bewildered helplessness. With Maura the concept of shame meant nothing at all. She acted as if her own desires magnetized the world, and when you were close to her, she magnetized your moral compass too. It would be wrong to say that men in her orbit lost their willpower. They just came to want the same as she did. Her son had inherited much of the same power, but he was at least aware of it. She was not. And while Bryan's friends set themselves self-consciously at an angle to the universe, Maura's followers felt the rest of the world tilting inexplicably since they'd found her.

She thought for a little, and then said urgently, 'Goodness won't suit Bryan, you understand.'

'How do you mean?'

'He can't spend the rest of his life taking care of her.'

'That's what the Colonel thinks.'

'But he would never say it – I know.'

'What am I supposed to do? I think Bryan's noble.'

She returned her attention to the road as if it made greater demands on her intelligence.

'I think you can take Paula off his hands while we talk.'

The road swung lazily past a caravan park. Most of the tide was out and the mudflats ahead of us glittered towards the fells that rose on the further shore. Bryan stopped his taxi on the seafront – a strip of road with a concrete barrier on one side and a line of whitewashed shops on the other. Maura pulled the gold car up behind and looked at us encouragingly while we levered out the wheelchair.

There was a wind off the sea, which smelt of mud and salt. As I breathed it in I seemed to swell with power and greed and lust for life. I looked down at Paula.

'FUCK!' she said. 'This is just . . . fucking wonderful. I have nae been here since the accident. Remember when we ran along the seafront, sweetie?'

'After they threw me out of the chippy? That was bad. All I did was ask why there was a sign in the alley outside saying "Beware of the dog" when it should have said "Beware of the steak pie". Same thing in the end.'

'Not bad for someone so drunk we almost had to drag him out after that.'

'But when the woman's sons came out – do you remember how we ran?'

'I want to run again,' Paula said, and something in the sea air filled me so I answered before anyone else could.

'I'll take you! Get on my back.'

Bryan and Maura hoisted Paula up and placed her legs on each side of my waist so that it looked like an ordinary piggyback. I started down the rough concrete of the seafront, heading north in the direction of Kendal, and beyond that Scotland. Half a mile on, the railway cut across on a long viaduct to Grange-over-Sands, the town on the other side.

'Come on! Take me to the end.'

She was extremely uncomfortable to carry. Only now did I understand how much a piggyback depends on the strength and cooperation of the piggy. I bent my own back to distribute her inert weight across my shoulders and set off. My stride seemed at first too long but after a hundred yards or so I felt strength moving into my legs and tried to straighten up.

'Giddy up!' said Paula, and giggled.

I broke into a shamble, then a grotesque, high-stepping jog. Her hair flapped around my neck and I smelt her sharp sweat mingling with my own. I felt the salt air filling me, and a fierce exhilaration that I was alive and could still run. I ran to celebrate this triumphal fact.

A short time later, I could not go on.

'Go on!' cried Paula. 'This is great!'

'I can't. My arms just hurt too much. I'm not used to carrying things.'

She panted against my neck, clenching her arms hard against my shoulders. 'Well, turn round then. But I hate it when people think I want to be calm. I never did want to be calm before. I don't want to be a vegefucking – oh fuck, fucking vegetable now. I –'

My feet seemed heavier on the way back. My legs hurt more but I made myself run anyway.

As we approached the other two, Bryan was staring at the ground. Maura looked out to sea. Neither spoke. Bryan looked up as we arrived. He was pale, even making allowances for a hangover.

He didn't ask his mother to help when we lowered Paula into the wheelchair.

'Anyone for ice cream?' he said. 'Come on, Andrew. You look as if you need it. Paula too.'

The front was deserted so late in the season, but the shops were still open. 'Don't bother for me. I'd rather have a cigarette,' said Maura.

It was impossible to get the wheelchair into the little ice-cream parlour. When we emerged, Maura had smoked half her cigarette and seemed to have got her strength back after whatever had passed between her and Bryan earlier. As soon as we were arranged in line and out of the wind, she spoke. 'People say I'm selfish but I am actually just reasonable. I know what the world is like and how little we can change it.'

Paula broke the silence that followed. She was never afraid of anything for long. 'People change the world in different ways. You certainly couldn't have carried me down the front. That changed mine.'

'Ah, Paula, if you have to trust in lawyers, you're fucked already!' She laughed. 'The ones who handled my divorce were useless.'

Bryan's face didn't twitch. He'd heard it all too many times before, but his body seemed to shrink a little further inside the lean black overcoat he wore. He said, 'Why don't we go and get a drink? There's a pub in Carnforth where they'll let our Paula in. You two can follow us again.'

At the pub he left me to manoeuvre Paula over the lintel while he charged ahead. I think he'd had two doubles before the rest of us emerged from the passage into the stone-flagged bar. There were no other customers. Dusty shafts of solid sunlight slanted across the deal tables, and the old leather sofas sagged against the wall. He let his mother buy us all a round. Paula drank lemonade; Maura, gin and tonic. I had a pint and Bryan a half-and-half. 'It's damn cold out there,' he said as a sort of explanation. We were still all at the bar when he turned to us.

'I don't think we want lunch with you, Mother. It's very kind of you to come all this way. But you don't enjoy our quaint rustic ways. I am not going to abandon Paula. I can perfectly well work here, and I don't need to be in London. I don't want to be in London, in fact. And even if there is nothing I can do to change the world, I would rather do that nothing in your company, sweetness.'

His hand had fallen to Paula's shoulder as he spoke. She, who might once have placed her hand on his, now simply stared at Maura, whose face was picked out pale gold in a sunbeam.

She put her drink down, half finished on the bar, and just as we braced ourselves for a chilling blast, she gave him a smile of quite unforced affection. 'It's your life,' she said, as if a difficult problem had just been solved. 'And I can't do anything more, for any of you.' She stubbed out her cigarette and left. ∎

Spelling Problem

A woman from Barnard College calls me and in the course of our phone conversation she asks me if I would please spell 'hemorrhaging' for her. I spell it, but wrong – maybe 'hemmhoraging'.

I don't like not knowing how to spell a word, since I am interested in how words are spelled.

So then I become curious and begin asking friends and others to spell that word – whenever I am talking to someone on the phone.

R. spells it 'hemmorhaging'.

E. spells it 'hemmoraging' and then hastily changes it to 'hemorhaging'.

Mother spells it 'hemorhaging'.

Mother, before spelling it, mentions the 'hae-' and 'he-' choice, which E. also mentioned.

At first I think the 'ae-' question is a 'red herring', as I say to E. (or a 'raed haerring'). But when I try writing the word using the 'ae-' form, I think maybe it isn't irrelevant after all. Maybe using the 'ae-' form would make it easier to spell the rest of the word correctly.

D. spells it 'hemmoraging'.

S. spells it 'hemhorraging'.

Ann L. spells it 'hemhoraging'.

But all this happened fifteen years ago. And although I keep thinking back and trying to remember, I just can't remember why a woman telephoning me from Barnard College would ask me to spell the word 'hemorrhaging'. ■

A HAND
REACHED DOWN
TO GUIDE ME

David Gates

The name Paul Thompson won't mean any more to you than my name would, but if you'd been around the bluegrass scene in New York some thirty years ago, you would have heard the stories. Jimmy Martin had wanted to make him a Sunny Mountain Boy, but he'd refused to cut his hair. He'd turned Kenny Baker on to pot at Bean Blossom, and played a show with Tony Trischka while tripping on acid. Easy to believe it all back then. The first time I actually saw him he was onstage, wearing a full-length plaster cast on his – give me a second to visualize this – his left leg, holding himself up by a crutch in each armpit, playing mandolin with only his forearms moving. And someone had Magic-Markered the bottom of the cast to look like an elephantine tooled-leather cowboy boot. This was at an outdoor contest in Roxbury, Connecticut, in 1977, the summer I turned eighteen. The band I'd come with had finished its two numbers, and we were behind the stage, putting instruments in cases when Paul kicked off 'Rawhide'. I heard our mandolin player say, 'Okay, we're fucked.'

His band – older longhairs, except the fiddle player, a scary guy with a Marine buzz cut – won first prize, as they had the year before. But we placed second, and he lurched over to me on his crutches and said he'd liked the way I'd sung 'Over in the Gloryland'. It was *Paul Thompson* saying this. I suppose I was a good singer, for a kid just out of high school; I thought of Christian songs simply as genre pieces in those days, but I had the accent down. I said, 'Thanks, man,' and refrained from embarrassing myself by complimenting him back. We ended up singing a few songs together out by the cars – I remember him braced up against somebody's fender – and I think it surprised him that I knew so much Louvin Brothers stuff: 'Too Late', 'Here Today and Gone Tomorrow', 'Are You Afraid to Die?'. I let him sing Ira's tenor parts; now that he'd stopped smoking, he said, he could get up there in the real keys. He was taller than me, and his cheekbones made him look like a hard-luck refugee in a Dust Bowl photograph; he had white hairs in his sideburns, though he must only have been in his thirties. He told me he'd broken the leg playing squash; naturally I thought it was a joke.

We'd both come up from the city that afternoon, me in a van with the banjo player in my band and his wife and kids, Paul driven by his girlfriend. As we were packing up, he asked me how I was getting back, and could I drive stick. The girlfriend got pissed at him, he said, and went off on the back of somebody's motorcycle, and now here he was up in East Buttfuck, Connecticut, and no way to get himself home. His car turned out to be an old TR6, with so much clutter behind the seats we had to tie my guitar to the luggage rack with bungee cords; all the way back to New York he played the Stanley Brothers on ninety-minute cassettes he'd dubbed from his LP collection. We didn't talk much – I had to wake him up to ask directions once we hit the West Side Highway – but I did note that he said *man*dolin, not mando*lin*, and I've taken care to say *man*dolin ever since.

He lived in a big old building on West End around 86th; because it was Saturday night I had no trouble finding a space on his block. He said he'd figure out some way to deal with the car on Monday. Did I want to come up, have a few more tunes, smoke some dope? He hadn't given *that* up. But it was late to be taking my guitar on the subway, and I already had enough of a Paul Thompson story to tell.

M ost of us were just weekend pickers, and only little by little did you learn about other people's real lives. Our banjo player taught calculus at Brooklyn College; the fiddler in Paul's band (the one native Southerner I ever ran across in New York) managed a fuel-oil business in Bay Ridge; another guy you saw around, good Dobro player, was a public defender. I was working in a bookstore that summer before starting NYU, where I planned to major in English. And Paul Thompson turned out to be a science writer at *Newsweek*. One day I saw him in the subway at Rockefeller Center, and I had to think a minute to figure out where I knew him from: he was wearing a blue oxford shirt and a seersucker blazer, with jeans and cowboy boots. Somebody told me he'd published a novel when he was in his twenties, which you could still find at the Strand.

A couple of years later, Paul brought me into his band when their lead singer moved to California, and we also played some coffee houses as a duet, calling ourselves the Twofer Brothers. I went to the University of Connecticut for graduate school but I drove down to the city a couple of times a month, and every so often Paul would put the band back together for some party where they'd place hay bales around the room. After these gigs we'd go up to his place, get high and listen to music, or drink and talk books. He told me he loved 'Jimmy Hank', and gave me a copy of *The Ambassadors* from his collection of pristine old Signet paperbacks; it had a price of fifty cents. By then I'd decided to specialize in the nineteenth century, and I resented Jimmy Hank for his review of *Our Mutual Friend* – 'poor with the poverty not of momentary embarrassment, but of permanent exhaustion'. But I've still got that book: the cover illustration shows a top-hatted gent seen from behind in a cafe chair, with wine glass and cane. I imagine it'll be on my shelves, still unread, when I die.

While I was finishing my dissertation, I got married to the first woman I'd ever lasted with for more than a month. Diane, I might as well admit, was my student when I was a TA, and why bother trying to extenuate it, all these years later, by telling you that we started sleeping together only after the semester was over? Or that in our History-of-Us conversations, we could never decide who'd made the first move? She'd go to festivals and parties with me to be the cool girlfriend with the cut-off jeans, and we promised each other that when we got out of married-student housing we'd live in the country somewhere, in a house full of books, no TV, and raise our own food.

I'd grown up in Park Slope, but my father was an old folkie – he used to hang around Washington Square in the fifties – and when I was twelve or thirteen I began listening to his LPs and fixating on the photos of ruined grampaws on their falling-down porches; even the mean, sad bluegrass guys in business suits and Stetsons, holding thousands of dollars' worth of Martins and Gibsons, had been posed by abandoned shacks in the mountains. Everybody in our little scene thought of themselves as secret country boys. My old banjo player, the one I rode up to Roxbury with, quit his teaching job and moved to the Northeast Kingdom, where I hear he makes B-string benders in his machine shop and plays pedal steel in a country band. Our bass player left the East Village for Toast, North Carolina, to sit at the feet of Tommy Jarrell. Even my father, in his bourgie-folkie way. He was an engineer at Con Edison for thirty years; when he retired he and my mother built a solar house up near Woodstock.

I found a teaching job at a small college in New Hampshire and Diane got accepted at the New England Culinary Institute. We bought a fixer-upper farmhouse, with a wood stove, a barn and twenty acres, on a dirt road, equally inconvenient to my school and hers. I put a metal roof on the old henhouse – Diane had always wanted to keep chickens – rototilled our garden patch every spring and bought a chainsaw and a splitter, as well as a rusty Ford 8N, the pretext being that we needed to keep the fields from growing back to brush. Our neighbour, a man in his seventies, kept the thing going for me; he liked us because I was so helpless and Diane was so pretty. In the spring he and I would work up the next winter's wood together, sharing my splitter and running his buzz saw off the tractor's PTO. I don't know how I did all this while teaching three and three and working on my book; when the old man finally went into a home I started buying cordwood. My parents drove up a couple of times a year, and my father always brought his single-O Martin, the guitar on which he taught me my first chords. He and I would sit around playing the half-dozen finger-picking songs – 'Lewis Collins', 'Spike Driver's Moan' – that he'd never cared to get beyond. They seldom stayed more than a day or two. The wood stove didn't keep the guest room warm enough in fall or winter, and my mother got bitten to death by mosquitoes in the summer.

Every July Diane and I threw an outdoor music party and pig roast; she'd cook the whole week before, and her friends from Boston and my friends from New York brought tents and sleeping bags and tried to dance to the ad-hoc bands that formed in the corners of the field behind the house. Paul Thompson always turned up with his mandolin, some good weed and a younger woman, never the same one twice.

For a few years, he'd drive that summer's woman to catch a bus in White River Junction and stay on until Tuesday or Wednesday. Diane liked him – what woman didn't, at first? – and he was no trouble to have around. He took walks in the woods by himself; he spent hours reading in the hammock on the porch, and didn't mind when we went up to bed and left him downstairs with his weed and his headphones. 'A man could die happy up here,' he used to say. He told me he liked hearing the rooster at first light, because it made him feel safe to go back to sleep. When he finally got up, he'd go out to the henhouse, gather eggs and cook his own breakfast – and clean up afterwards. Diane usually picked eggs early in the morning, but she'd leave a couple for him to find. Once, when he'd been out there for what seemed like a long time, I went to check on him, and I saw him through the window, squatting on his hams, his cowboy boots the only part of him touching the floor. He was talking and nodding to himself, or to the hens, who came right up to him as they never did for me. I sneaked back to the house and I don't think he heard me.

But most of the time, Paul wasn't anybody I thought about much, though I know now that he was thinking about me.

For whatever reason, I never wanted children. Not a crime against humanity – arguably quite the opposite – but of course this became an issue when Diane turned thirty. That and suspicions about me and my students, which I should have seen coming as well, and about one student in particular. (The wrong one, as it happened.) Diane and I lasted ten years, and after she left I drank myself to sleep every night for a month. Didn't that argue that I wasn't cold-hearted? She's remarried now, has her own catering business, and her older daughter's applying to colleges – better schools than the one where I teach. We're on good enough terms these days that she sends me pictures. At the time of the divorce, though, she held out for money in return for her share in the house, and I had no prospect of a better-paying job. My book, *Cathy's Caliban: Sex, Race and the Sublime in Wuthering Heights* – a rewrite of my dissertation – got only one notice, in *Victorian Studies*, whose reviewer (from some other no-name college, in Missouri) called it 'by turns perverse and pedestrian'. The book got me tenure, since nobody else in the department had published in the past ten years, but only a two-thousand-dollar raise. So I went back to working up my own wood, until – God, must we? – Until I was able to sell my father's house.

Diane had already left the last time he came up, the fall after my mother died. He had his Martin with him, as usual, but he didn't feel like playing. Could he leave it with me? The strings felt stiff; maybe I could take it to the guy who worked on my guitar? It didn't feel any different to me, but I told him I'd see if Brad could bring the action down a little. Hell, I thought, he's seventy-eight, his fingers might not be as strong as they used to be. This turned out to be what Harold Bloom might call a weak misreading.

I set the chessboard up on the wooden factory spool Diane and I had used for a coffee table – he mostly kicked my ass – and poured glasses of the Jameson he always brought. While I was considering whether or not to move a rook, he picked up a photo from the table beside the sofa: Diane and I sitting at a cafe in Barcelona, the one time we went to Europe.

'What are you, running a museum?' he said. 'Look, I liked Diane. Your mother had her opinion, fine. Me, I think you were crazy to let her go. But you made your choice, right?'

'You *could* call it that.'

'And you still got all her hair shit in there.' He flipped his thumb in the direction of the bathroom, where Diane had left behind mostly empty bottles of conditioners, moisturizers and lotions.

'Don't think I don't see what you're up to.'

'What, throw you off your game? You fucked yourself two moves back.' I looked the board over again, then got up and put another couple of logs in the stove.

'What I'd do?' he said. 'Find some sucker who wants to be – who'm I trying to think of? Thoreau. Then buy yourself a nice little place where you don't have to do *that* nine months a year. You want to be living like this when you're my age?'

'I seem to recall you couldn't wait to get out of the city.'

'Not to live like a sharecropper. You even get cable up here?'

'We don't have a TV.' I sat down again and took another look at the board.

'Interesting,' he said. 'And who's the "we"?'

'Yeah, okay. I get it.'

'Anyway, now your mother's gone and I'm staring at trees all day. You could have a life. You meeting anybody?'

I laid my king on its side. 'Pop. It's been a month.'

'That's my point.' He looked out the window. 'These trees are gonna kill you.'

By the time Janna moved in, I'd been living in New Hampshire for longer than I had in the city, though I still wasn't fooling the locals any. You could see another house by then: an A-frame up on the rise catty-corner across the road. Diane and I could have bought that parcel along with the land on this side, but we hadn't been able to come up with the extra ten thousand dollars. I hated to look over there.

Janna worked at Century 21, near my college in the old downtown. Yes, I met her at the bar where I'd started going after classes. She'd gotten her job just by walking in and asking for it, and her boss liked the tricks she'd picked up on some website: putting bowls of lemons and Granny Smith apples on kitchen counters, fanning out copies of *Country Journal* on coffee tables. I thought she was too bright to have ended up here: she had an MA in political science from Tufts. But she said she'd found her place in the world. I suppose I had too.

She told me right from the beginning that she didn't want to be the Second Wife, and she'd put a bumper sticker on her Subaru reading COPULATE DON'T POPULATE.

Her apartment had track lighting, good oriental rugs and a gas fireplace, but she seemed to feel at home in my house. Aside from repainting the living room – a yellow she said would feel warmer than the white Diane and I had gone with – all she did was move the sofa over to where the armchair had been, and find us a pine blanket chest for a coffee table. She was fine with dial-up and no TV – she'd let corporate media waste too much of her time, she said – and she even claimed the rooster didn't wake her, though she refused to go into the henhouse herself. After five years, we still had sex more days than not: I'd made peace with her chubby knees; presumably she'd made peace with my loose belly and my too-small hands.

Janna played guitar – another point in her favour – and we sang together once in a while. I'd back her up on her songs – Ani DiFranco, Michelle Shocked, the Indigo Girls, some of it not as bad as you might think – and she knew 'Silver Threads and Golden Needles' and the usual stuff by Emmylou Harris. I tried to teach her a couple of Porter and Dolly songs, though she didn't have much of a range and we could never hit on the right key for her. It was Janna, in fact, who talked me into having the music parties again. She hated to cook, so we'd lay in beer and Jack Daniel's and chips, get pizzas delivered and tell people to bring whatever. She hung back most of the time and let the bluegrass guys do their inside-baseball thing – *Yeah, 'Rank Strangers'. Who's gonna do Ralph's part?* – but late at night I could sometimes get her to step into a circle of pickers and sing 'Sin City'.

'We could probably make this work,' she'd told me when we'd been together for a month. 'If neither of us turns into an asshole.'

'How likely is that?' I said.

'Well,' she said, 'if people aren't willing to change. I mean when things call for it.'

'But you're happy *now*.'

'You would've heard,' she said.

When I sent the notice out for the party that last summer – we were having it early, since we were going to Yorkshire in July, to see the Brontë country – Paul emailed back that he'd taken a buyout from *Newsweek* and was 'living on Uneasy Street', but that he'd try to make it. He was working on a book proposal, he said, about mountaintop removal, which would get him some time in eastern Kentucky – where maybe he'd be able to play some music too, if he didn't show up in a car with New York plates.

The Friday night of the party, he rolled into the dooryard just after dark, in a Jeep Wrangler, with a woman at the wheel. She looked to be Janna's age, and not quite up to Paul's standards – maybe too much nose and too little chin – but with a slender body and straight, dyed-black hair down to her shoulders. He got out, stretched and looked off at the hills. 'Shee-*it!*' he said to the woman. 'Just smell the air. I ever tell you? This is my favourite place in the world.'

'Several times,' she said.

'I want y'all to meet Simone,' he said. He always talked more Southern when he was around the music. 'My last and best.'

'Until the rest of the ass parade comes around the corner.' She ran a finger down his arm.

'Never happen,' Paul said. He looked even lankier than usual, and when he turned to me I saw dark pouches pulling his eyelids down, exposing red below his eyeballs. 'Hey, listen, we gotta do "Hit Parade of Love". But first off – what do you say?' He opened his mandolin case and took out a pipe and a plastic bag of buds.

After one hit, I knew I'd had plenty, and that a beer might help and might not; even Paul stopped at three. He kicked off 'Hit Parade of Love', and somehow I found myself singing the first verse, whose words I thought until the last instant wouldn't come to me – *From what I been a-hearin', dear, you really got it made* – but when we got to the chorus, with the tenor part, his voice cracked on the word *top*, and he asked if we could take it down to A. Well, hell, he had to be what, pushing seventy by now? If I was fifty-one?

He gave up before midnight – he said the drive had done him in – and we put him and Simone in the big guest room at the far end of the hall. When the music petered out around two thirty and people retired to their tents and RVs, Janna and I came upstairs and saw their light was still on; Janna thought she heard him coughing. The rooster woke me for a few seconds as the windows began to show grey; I hoped that if Paul was hearing it too he'd fall back safe asleep.

In the morning I put on one of the knee-length white aprons Diane had left behind, cooked up enough scrambled eggs, along with kale from the garden, to fill the turkey-roasting pan, set out paper plates and plastic forks and clanged the triangle she'd always used to get the party guests in. Paul and Simone didn't come down until the others were finishing up. 'You sleep okay?' I said.

'Never better,' he said. The pouches under his eyes looked darker in daylight. 'Once I got my *nightly obligations* taken care of.' He put a hand on Simone's ass and squeezed. 'This is the one that's gonna be the death of me.'

'You'll scandalize your friend,' she said. 'Look how he's blushing.'

Paul reached down, lifted the hem of my apron and peeked under. 'What's fer breakfast, Maw?'

They took plates out onto the porch, and when I came out after a preliminary clean-up, I found Janna sitting next to him while Simone was on the lawn trying to get up into a headstand, her black hair splashed out on the grass. He hadn't touched his eggs. 'Hey, the Iron Chef,' he said. 'Listen, did I tell you I'm playing bass in a rock band? Like one of those daddy bands? I fuckin' love it – we missed so much shit being hillbillies.' He speared a forkful of egg, but set it down. 'I might have to quit, though.'

'What's going on with the book?'

'Yeah, well, that too. Story for another time.' Simone had gotten both feet in the air, muscled legs straight, toes pointed, black-polished toenails. Paul clapped his hands and called 'Brava!' He turned back to me. 'I can't believe I finally got it right,' he said. 'In the bottom of the ninth. Check her the fuck out.'

'She seems great,' I said. The legs of Simone's shorts had fallen just enough to expose about that much of black lacy underwear.

'Listen, I might call you pretty soon to ask you a favour,' he said. 'I *might*. It would be a *big* favour.' He looked at Janna. 'From both of you.'

'*You're* being mysterious,' she said.

'Sure,' I said. 'Whatever whenever.'

'I appreciate it.' He stood up and called to Simone. 'You going to stay like that all day, babe? Come on, I want to show you the gals.'

He took her hand and led her along the path to the henhouse. He was limping worse than usual – that broken leg had never healed properly – and I noticed that he was wearing Nikes instead of boots.

Janna touched my arm. 'I don't think he's okay.'

'He's just in love,' I said.

'I could see that little display wasn't lost on you.' I was thinking of how to deny it, but she put a finger to my lips. 'I mean, you know him better than I do,' she said, 'but *I* think she's got a situation on her hands.'

That summer was the first time Janna and I had travelled together. The Brontë Trail turned out to be a five-hour trudge through British badlands – 'No wonder the brother was an alcoholic,' Janna said – and back in Haworth we found our rental car had a yellow metal clamp on the front wheel. At Whitby, it was too cold to swim, and neither of us had any interest in joining the fossil-hunters at low tide, or in taking the Dracula tour. When we got home, I found a package Janna had sent me from Amazon – she'd found an Internet cafe in Whitby – with a book of Doré's illustrations of the *Divine Comedy*, and a note reading *It's time we got you interested in writers from Tuscany*.

A week later, I got the email.

This is Simone, Paul's friend. I hope you remember me from your party. He doesn't know I'm writing this (truly), but I was afraid he never would ask you. I'm sure you must have seen that he wasn't well, and the truth is that he's been diagnosed with liver cancer, stage 4, though he still seems like his old self most days. Anyway, I know that his wish is, and I apologize if this is just too much to ask, that you could let him be in your home for the very last part of this – he says he will know when. He has always told me your home was his favourite place ever to be. I can take care of all the arrangements, home hospice and etc (truth is, I've already made some calls to places in your area). Not really knowing you, I hope I've explained all this in the right way. Do you think you could in any way do this for him?

'What?' Janna said. We were propped up together on the bed. One thing I'd learned from being married to Diane was not to be furtive about email.

'Here.' I turned the screen her way. 'I guess you called it.'

I watched her face as she read, but Janna didn't give much away. 'He put her up to this,' she said.

'She says not.'

'Well of course,' she said. 'That's the tell.'

'I just have no idea what to say to something like this.'

'He's your friend,' she said. 'What time is it?'

'So you're saying I should call?'

'I don't even know this man,' she said. 'But I'd do this with you.'

They came late on a Sunday afternoon in October. Simone helped him out of the Jeep, then reached behind the seat and handed Janna a gallon of cider, just as she might have done if they'd been normal lovers up for a country weekend. The label showed it was the catchpenny orchard on the state highway, where kids could feed donkeys with pellets from dispensing machines at a quarter a handful. Paul had let his beard grow in, entirely white; he looked like the last pictures of Ezra Pound. 'And here he is,' he said. 'Appearing for a limited time only.'

'He rehearses his lines,' Simone said.

Janna put him on the sofa with the afghan over him while Simone and I went back out to get his stuff. 'It's just a few clothes,' Simone said, 'and a couple of pictures he wanted to be able to look at. He didn't want to take up your space. I think he's planning to give you this.' She held up the mandolin case.

'That's crazy,' I said. 'It's got to be worth a fortune.' Paul's F-5 wasn't a Lloyd Loar, but I remembered that it was from the thirties.

'Welcome to my life,' she said. 'He tried to leave *me* his apartment. He's turned into the Bill and Melinda Gates Foundation. I have to get with his brother tomorrow in the city and figure out what to do. Paul won't talk to him.'

'You're not driving down again tonight?'

'Breakfast 8 a.m. The brother's a freak too.'

'But you're coming back.'

'And you've known Paul for how long? I mean, I wanted to. He's got it all plotted out, like each of us with our own little jobs – I mean, not that yours is little. He's just putting everybody away, away, away. Fuck *him*, you know? I was a good girlfriend.'

'Would you like us to disappear for a while? We do need to go to the store at some point.'

'No, it's fine. He already got the last sweet blow job. Under this fucking apple tree – sorry. I just feel like *somebody* should know. And all the way up here, he keeps finding these sports-talk stations. Did you know that the World Series begins next week? It's going to be quite a match-up.'

We found him sitting up on the sofa, propped up by pillows under his back, looking at the *New York Review of Books*. 'So,' he said, 'did she tell you what a dick I'm being to her?'

'I can imagine how hard this must be for both of you,' I said.

'Ah, still the slick-fielding shortstop,' he said. 'But we're into serious October baseball here.'

'Can you just *stop*?' Simone said.

'Isn't that the whole idea?' he said.

Janna came downstairs with her arms full of sheets and blankets. 'We're going to put you guys in the den tonight,' she said. 'I thought it would be easier than having to do stairs.'

'She has to go back,' I said.

'You know,' Paul said. 'Stuff to do with the, ah, e, s, t, a, t, e.'

Simone turned to me. 'They said they'd be coming with the bed tomorrow morning. And the nurse should be here. You have my information, right?'

Paul shook his finger at her. 'Now *that* should have been said sotto voce.'

'Let me make you some coffee,' Janna said. 'I don't know if anything's open between here and the interstate.'

'She'll be cool,' Paul said. 'My guy brought over some Adderall before we left. He gets the *real* stuff. Made from adders.'

I walked Simone out to the car. She opened the driver's door, then turned back and came into my arms, taking deep breaths. 'He's been lucky to have you,' I said.

'And now he's lucky to have you,' she said. 'There's just no end to his luck.'

In bed that night, I said to Janna, 'Can we really do this?'

'What's our choice at *this* point?' We were lying on our backs, and she rolled over, her breasts against my arm. 'Did you two talk at all?'

'I don't want to, you know, press him.' I worked my arm over her shoulder and pulled her closer. Her belly into my hip. She sighed and moved her palm up my thigh.

'Why didn't he ever, you know, find somebody?' she said. I felt myself beginning to get hard – could we really do *this*? 'That woman loves him.'

'He never had any trouble *finding* them,' I said.

'Do you ever wish you were like him?'

'What, you mean dying?'

She jerked away and rolled onto her back again. 'I hate when you pretend to be stupid.'

'No,' I said. 'Who would ever want a life *that* lonely?'

'It's even more obnoxious when you try to figure out the right thing to say.'

I shoved a pillow against the headboard and sat up. 'Are we fighting?' I said. 'Because this is a hell of a time for it.'

'For the record, I don't blame you for getting us into this. I just hope it gets over with quickly. Is that horrible to say?'

'No, it's actually the *kindest* thing you could say.'

'But would you say it about me? If *I* were in the situation?'

'Come on,' I said. 'Nobody can ever –'

'Okay, I need to go to sleep,' she said. 'Obviously I'm not going to get laid tonight. Why don't you go down and check on your friend and see if he's still breathing. Then you can get yourself a drink and forget all about it.'

I put my legs over the side and got to my feet. 'I bring you one?'

'I'll be asleep,' she said. 'You don't even listen any more.'

The rooster woke me at six. I heard Janna breathing away and couldn't get back to sleep. But when I came downstairs Paul had already dressed himself, except for shoes and socks – he'd told us it hurt to bend down – and had managed to get from the den, where Janna had made up the fold-out, to the living-room sofa, and was stretched out listening to something through earbuds. He flicked them out when he saw me.

'How are you?' I said. 'You hurting? I can get you another Vicodin.'

'Just took a couple. They're coming with the real shit this morning, right?'

'They should be here by ten,' I said.

'What we like to hear. Listen, did I even thank you for this?'

'You'd do it for me.'

'*There's* a hypothetical we won't be putting to the test. Man, I have been such a shit. To everybody in my life.'

'You were never a shit to me,' I said.

'You weren't *in* my life. Well, who the fuck was. Not to be grim.

How did I get onto this? That Vicodin must work better than I thought. Your lady still asleep?'

'She was.'

He nodded. 'She's going to need it.'

I was in the kitchen cutting up a pineapple when I heard Janna come downstairs. She must have smelled the coffee brewing. 'You boys are up bright and early,' she said.

'Only way to live a long and healthy life,' Paul said. 'Get up, do the chores, plough the north forty – I don't mean anything sexual by that.'

'No, I'm sure that's the *last* thing you'd think of.' She came into the kitchen and put a hand on my arm. 'Did you get enough sleep? I'm sorry I was being . . . whatever I was.'

I set the knife down and put an arm around her. 'I think you get a free pass, considering.'

'I hope I was just getting it out of my system early.' She poured a cup of coffee, and put in milk for me. 'Will you be okay with him if I go in for a while? I should get some stuff done while I can.'

'Hey,' Paul yelled out. 'Why's everybody talking behind the patient's back?'

'Shut up, we're having sex,' she called back. She poured a cup for herself. 'He seems pretty chipper this morning.'

'Yeah, I don't know what to hope for,' I said. 'Quality, I guess. And then not too much quantity.'

A little after nine they came with the hospital bed, and the guy helped me move the sofa into the corner so we could set the bed up in the living room, by the window looking out at the hills. Janna and I would take the fold-out in the den when it became clear that we had to be nearby. Paul watched us from the armchair, his bare feet on a footstool, his earbuds back in, his eyes on us. When the guy left, he turned the iPod off, plucked out the earbuds and said, 'Why am I reminded of "In the Penal Colony"?'

The FedEx truck delivered a cardboard box with the drugs, then the nurse from the hospice showed up. She had thick black hair, going grey, down her back in a single braided pigtail, and hoop earrings – not what you'd expect with the white uniform. Her name was Heather. I brought her a mug of herbal tea – she wasn't a coffee drinker, she said – and she showed me the spreadsheet-looking printed forms, on which we were to record dosage and time, then opened the FedEx box, picked up her clipboard and took inventory. She wrote down Paul's temperature and blood pressure, listened to his heart. 'So, Paul,' she said, 'how would you say your pain is right now?'

'One to ten? Let's give it a seven. Good beat and you can dance to it.'

'We can improve on that,' she said.

'Can you do less than zero?'

'That's going to be up to you. And your caregivers. I'm a believer that you keep on top of the pain. This shouldn't be about you being in any discomfort.' She got up and put on her jacket – wool, with a Navajo design. 'I'll be by tomorrow, but if you have any concerns or questions, any emergency, someone's always there.'

I took my jacket off the coat rack. 'Here, I'll walk you out. I've got to feed the hens.'

'Smooth,' Paul said. 'Jesus Christ, why don't you just ask her how long?'

'I knew I was going to like you,' she said to him. 'I'll be seeing you tomorrow – that much I think we can count on.'

I followed her to her car. 'I'm not asking you to make a prediction,' I said. 'But just from your experience.'

'Okay, based on nothing? I think he'll move fast.'

When I came back in he was sitting on the edge of the hospital bed, bare feet dangling, pushing the button and making it go up and down. 'So, we going to break out the good stuff?'

'Should you wait till what she gave you kicks in?'

'Don't start *that*,' he said. 'You heard the lady.' He lay back, stuck out his tongue and pointed at it.

He dozed – call it that – until the middle of the afternoon, while I sat in the armchair, checking from time to time to make sure his chest was rising and falling, and making notes in my new paperback copy of *Middlemarch*; the covers had finally come off my old one. If Janna could hold the fort tomorrow while I went in to campus, that's what I'd be teaching.

'Let's go for a ride.' I looked up: Paul's eyes were open. 'I want to see some trees, man. And can we bring some music? I got weed.'

'If you're up to it,' I said. 'Stanley Brothers? You remember driving back from Roxbury that time?'

'Not really,' he said. 'Did I have that fucked-up Triumph?'

'Yeah. Whatever became of that?'

'Whatever became of anything? I should've kept a journal. Fucking *years* of fucking lost days.'

The truck had a handle above the door frame that you could grab to pull yourself up onto the seat; Paul used both hands, but I still had to take his legs and hoist. I could feel the bones.

We took back roads, dirt roads when I could find them. Cornfields with ranks of tubular stubble, falling-down barns, with Holsteins standing outside in the mud. Hunting season had started – that morning I'd heard gunshots in the woods – and we passed a double-wide where a buck hung from a kids' swingset, one front hoof scraping the ground.

'My kind of place,' he said. 'You know, when they say you're dead meat – like isn't meat dead by definition?' He snapped the buck a salute. 'Shit, *I* should have settled up here. Come to think of it, I *have* settled up here.'

'I always thought *you'd* get a place out of the city. At least for weekends.'

'I think it would have ruined it,' he said. 'I was really just into the songs. Hey, can we have the Stanleys?'

'I just want to say,' I said. 'I admire the way you're dealing with this.'

'Yeah, wait till the screaming starts.'

I put in a Stanley Brothers CD – *Can't you hear the night bird crying?* – and he began packing a bowl. He blew out the first cloud of skunky smoke, then held it out to me. I put up my hand, and opened my window.

'You mind cracking yours just a little?' I said. 'If this is that shit you had last summer . . .'

'That? That was fucking ditchweed.' He exhaled again. 'Yeah, actually I wouldn't advise you.' He closed his eyes. 'Okay. Better. I haven't heard this for fucking ever.'

After a few miles, he packed the bowl again. 'What's so weird,' he said, 'I can't tell if something's beautiful any more. Like, is *that* beautiful?' He pointed at the CD player: the Stanley Brothers were singing 'My Sinful Past' – where the harmony comes in on *a hand reached down to guide me*.

'Well,' I said. 'I mean I'm not always in the mood.'

'Okay, you don't want to talk absolutes,' he said. 'Can't blame you there.'

We stopped at the convenience store outside of West Rumney – we'd run out of milk. 'Anything I can get you?' I said.

'I'm disappointing you,' he said. 'You want to know what this is like.'

'Not unless you want to tell me,' I said. 'This isn't about me.'

'Right, see that's my point,' he said. 'Listen, would they have eggnog this early? I mean in the year?'

'That's a thought.'

'Yes it is,' he said. 'Good for me, right? Could you leave the thing on?' We'd switched over to the King recordings; the Stanley Brothers were singing 'A Few More Years'.

But when I came out with the milk and a half-gallon of eggnog, already with holly wreath and red ribbon on the carton, he was sitting in silence. 'I didn't want to run down your battery,' he said. Could he have been crying? His eyes had looked red all day. And of course he'd been smoking. I had to help him get the eggnog open and hold the carton up so he could sip. 'How did Bob Cratchit drink this shit?' he said. 'Guess I can cross this off too.'

Back at the house, he lay on the sofa for a while, then got up, bent over, groaned and picked up the mandolin case. 'You know, I haven't played since your thing,' he said. 'I want you to have this.'

'Come on, buddy. I could never play mandolin for shit. There must be somebody who could really –'

'Fuck *somebody*,' he said.

Just two days later, he'd gotten so weak that Heather brought him a walker, which he used to get back and forth to the armchair and the bathroom. Then he stopped going to the armchair, and she brought in a commode; he could get his legs over the side of the bed, and if you'd bring the walker over he could get to his feet, go the two steps by himself, turn and sit, in his open-backed hospital johnny. And then Janna had to help him; he wouldn't let me. And then the bedpan. And then the day Heather came to catheterize him. He said to Janna, 'Here goes our last chance.' That was the same day Heather hooked him up to the morphine. Think of this as the baseline, she told us, and then you give him more by mouth. This is in your hands, she told us. You understand what I'm saying?

After our car ride, he never wanted music again. He'd brought pictures in stand-up Plexiglas frames: a photo of Simone, a postcard reproduction of Scipione Pulzone's *The Lamentation* (1591) – I looked at the back – and a snapshot of the two of us, standing in front of my house. I set them up on the table by his bed, but I never saw him look at them.

He screamed when we turned him to prevent bedsores – it took me and Janna together – but still insisted on being turned, until he didn't. When he could no longer drink, we swabbed the inside of his mouth with supposedly mint-flavoured sponges, the size of sugar cubes, on plastic sticks. At first he'd made faces at the taste of the morphine; then he was sucking at the dropper.

One day, the day before the last day, he motioned me to bend down and whispered, 'Why will you not just *do* it? They're not gonna say shit to you. *She* knows.'

'Buddy,' I said, 'you know I can't.' Which she was the *she*? He'd gotten to a point where he was conflating Heather and Janna.

'I'm not your buddy,' he said. 'You cocksucker.'

On his last night, we both slept in the living room with him – *slept*, I guess, isn't the word – Janna on the sofa, me on the floor, and took turns getting up every half-hour to dose him again. I'd stopped drawing the morphine up to the exact line on the dropper: just squirted in as much as it would hold, then watched the tip of his tongue touch at the green crust on his lips. I'd write down the time and *20mg*, hoping they wouldn't check my chart too carefully against what drugs would be left. When the light finally started going grey outside, I turned on his bedside lamp – I saw his eyelids tighten – gave him the next dropper, ten minutes early, then another one for good measure. In a while, the moaning quieted down; I turned the lamp off, went to the window and saw pink above the mountains. I pulled my fleece over my sweatshirt and went out to feed the hens. Frost on the grass, a faint quarter-moon still high.

Walking back to the house, I saw the light go on in the living room. Janna was standing over his bed, holding his hand, the one with the needle taped to it. 'Where *were* you?' she said. 'He was asking for you.'

I leaned over him; he was still breathing, but shallow breaths. 'Should we call them?' I said.

His eyes came open and he said, 'I've never been *here* before.'

'Don't be afraid,' Janna told him.

He rolled his head an inch one way, an inch the other. 'I don't know how to do this.'

'You can just let go,' she said.

'Oh fuck,' he said. 'You are one stupid twat.'

Janna's head jerked back, but she kept hold of his hand.

'Is there anything you want us to do?' I said.

He closed his eyes. 'You won't.' He began drawing harder, deeper breaths. 'I keep being mean,' he said.

'Rest,' I said. I took his other hand.

He rolled his head again. 'I need to get this right.'

Janna put her other hand on his, over where the needle went in.

'We both love you,' she said. 'It's okay to go.'

'I don't know,' he said.

We watched him breathe. It took longer and longer for the next one to come, and then there wasn't a next one.

I looked at Janna. She pointed back at him. You could see it: there was nobody in there any more.

I let go of the hand. 'I better call them.'

'Can't you take a *minute*?' she said. 'This is what he came to give you.'

After Heather left, and the guy from the funeral home took the body away in the back of his black Escalade, I drove Janna into town for breakfast. It was still only ten in the morning. There was a family in the next booth, so it must have been Saturday. Or Sunday. One of the kids was playing games on his phone or whatever; I could hear the little beeps and the snatches of metallic music. How could this not be driving the parents crazy? Janna ordered a grapefruit that she didn't eat; I had pancakes and no coffee. They were supposed to pick up the bed around noon, and I planned to sleep away the rest of the day.

'How are you holding up?' I said.

'He was absolutely right,' she said. 'I *am* a stupid twat. At least you kept your mouth shut. *We love you we love you we love you it's all right to go.* I'm going to be hearing that the rest of my life.'

'He didn't know what he was saying. We did the right thing for him.'

'So that's what you'd want? Somebody doing the *right thing* for you?'

'You're beating yourself up,' I said. 'We're both exhausted.'

'This has to change.' She pushed the grapefruit away and waved to get the waitress. 'Can you take me back to the house so I can get my car? Shit's been piling up at my office.'

'They can spare you for one more day.'

'You don't get what I'm telling you,' she said. 'I'm not spending another night there. You can do what you want. Wear her fucking aprons, feed her fucking chickens. Sing your dead-people songs, whatever. Read your dead-people books. You're going to kill yourself one of these days, making that drive in the winter. Look, this is my fault – I should have helped you. But you don't even know who I am.'

These days the summer parties happen in other people's fields, behind other people's farmhouses. So far this year I've been to one near Ludlow, Vermont, and another one an hour south of Albany. It's always the same people, give or take, and the same songs, said to be timeless. Our crowd isn't old enough yet to be dying off; they don't even seem to age that much year by year. But their kids, whose names I never remember, keep getting older, until you don't see them any more.

When I go, I go alone: Janna says if she has to hear a banjo one more time she'll shoot herself, and I'm grateful to her for saying so. I've given Paul's mandolin to the son of that banjo player, the guy I used to play with all those years ago. He's nineteen or twenty, the son, loves the music and has the gift; he'd been playing some hopeless Gibson knock-off. You still see one or two like him. He makes it to some of the parties and we'll do a song or two, I hope not just because he feels obliged. I suppose I'm getting too old to be standing out in a field on a summer night as the dew makes the strings slick, but I can still sing; having some age on me, maybe I sound more like the real thing.

It only took Janna two months to sell the old house on the dirt road. She got us our asking price, enough to buy a three-bedroom Craftsman-style bungalow – an office for her, a study for me – ten blocks from campus, four blocks from the health-food store. I walk to class, except on the coldest days, and Janna rides her bicycle to work. I play squash once a week with my department chair. We've bought a flat-screen television, forty-six inches, high definition, for my ball games and her shows. I'm making notes toward a second book. If I can ever finish, it could get me invited to a conference or two; despite that trip to the Brontë country, Janna says she wants to travel with me. You see all this as a defeat, I know. I would have. But I can't begin to tell you. ■

Ann Beattie's books include the story collections *What Was Mine* and *Follies*, the novel *Chilly Scenes of Winter* and the novella *Walks With Men*. She is the author of *Mrs. Nixon: A Novelist Imagines a Life* and a recipient of the PEN/Malamud Award.

Fiona Benson's first pamphlet was published as part of the Faber New Poets series. *Bright Travellers*, from which 'Toboggan Run' is taken, will be published by Jonathan Cape in May.

Andrew Brown's book about Sweden, *Fishing in Utopia*, won the 2009 Orwell Prize. He is working on a book about dying and another about religion.

Bernard Cooper's most recent book is *The Bill from My Father*. He is the recipient of the PEN/Hemingway Award, and fellowships from the Guggenheim Foundation and the National Endowment for the Arts. His work has appeared in five volumes of The Best American Essays series. 'My Avant-Garde Education' is an extract from a book of the same title, forthcoming from Norton.

Lydia Davis was awarded the 2013 Man Booker International Prize. Her most recent works include a translation of Gustave Flaubert's *Madame Bovary*; *The Cows*, a chapbook; and *Our Village*, a long poem in the chapbook *Two American Scenes*. Her new collection of stories, *Can't and Won't*, is published in April.

David Gates is the author of the novels *Jernigan* and *Preston Falls* and the story collection *The Wonders of the Invisible World*. He teaches at the University of Montana and in the Bennington Writing Seminars. 'A Hand Reached Down to Guide Me' is the title story of his forthcoming collection.

Aracelis Girmay is the author of the collage-based picture book *changing, changing* and the poetry collections *Teeth* and *Kingdom Animalia*, for which she was awarded a GLCA New Writers Award and the Isabella Gardner Award, respectively. She teaches in the School for Interdisciplinary Arts at Hampshire College.

Brigitte Grignet's photographs have been published in *Newsweek*, *El Pais* and *Le Monde* and have been included in the collections of the Kiyosato Museum of Photographic Arts, the Charleroi Museum of Photography and the Portland Art Museum.

Laura Kasischke has published eight novels and eight collections of poetry. Her most recent collection, *Space, in Chains*, received the National Book Critics Circle Award in 2011. She teaches at the University of Michigan.

Yuri Kozyrev began his career photographing the collapse of the Soviet Union. He photographed the wars in Iraq and Afghanistan for *Time* magazine, and since 2011 has been documenting the Arab uprisings and their aftermaths in the Middle East. 'Paradise Lost' appears courtesy of NOOR/eyevine.

Olivia Laing is a writer and critic. She is the author of *To the River* and *The Trip to Echo Spring* and is currently working on *The Lonely City*, a cultural history of urban loneliness.

Janet Malcolm's books include *Reading Chekhov, In the Freud Archives, The Journalist and the Murderer, Psychoanalysis: The Impossible Profession* and *Forty-One False Starts: Essays on Artists and Writers.*

Colin McAdam is the author of the novels *Some Great Thing, Fall* and *A Beautiful Truth.*

Lorrie Moore has recently retired from the University of Wisconsin. 'Thank You for Having Me' is taken from *Bark*, her fourth collection of stories, forthcoming from Knopf in the US and Faber & Faber in the UK.

Katherine Faw Morris is a native of north-west North Carolina. 'A Killing' is an extract from her debut novel *Young God*, forthcoming from Farrar, Straus and Giroux in the US and Granta Books in the UK.

Norman Rush is the author of *Whites, Mating* and *Mortals*. His fourth book, *Subtle Bodies*, was published in September.

Jonny Steinberg is the author of several books about South Africa's transition to democracy. His next book, *A Man of Good Hope*, will be published in January 2015. He teaches African Studies and Criminology at the University of Oxford.

Nathan Thornburgh is the co-founder of the online magazine *Roads & Kingdoms*. He is a former editor and foreign correspondent at *Time* magazine.

Marta Werner is a professor of English at D'Youville College in Buffalo, New York. Her works include *Emily Dickinson's Open Folios: Scenes of Reading, Surfaces of Writing* and *Radical Scatters: An Electronic Archive of Emily Dickinson's Late Fragments and Related Texts*. She has recently collaborated with the poet and artist Jen Bervin on *The Gorgeous Nothings*, a collection of the poems and other writings that Dickinson composed on envelopes.

Edmund White has written some twenty-five books – novels, memoirs, travel books, biographies and essays. 'American Vogue' is an extract from *Inside a Pearl: My Years in Paris*, published in February by Bloomsbury.

Joy Williams has written four novels, three story collections and *Ill Nature*, a book of essays. She was inducted into the American Academy of Arts and Letters in 2008.